OFF THE PEG ASSEMBLIES

30 fully worked-out sessions

CHRIS STAFFORD

kevin
mayhew

First published in 2004 by
KEVIN MAYHEW LTD
Buxhall, Stowmarket, Suffolk, IP14 3BW
E-mail: info@kevinmayhewltd.com
KINGSGATE PUBLISHING INC
1000 Pannell Street, Suite G, Columbia, MO 65201
E-mail: sales@kingsgatepublishing.com

Some assemblies are based on stories from *The Lion First Bible*, text
copyright © 1997 Pat Alexander.

Breakfast cereals and chocolate bars mentioned in assemblies 2 and 5
of 'The Life of Christ/the Christian life' are trademarked to their
respective owners.

Assembly 4 of 'The Lord's Prayer' is based on material published in
SALT resources © 1996 Scripture Union. Used with permission.

0 1 2 3 4 5 6 7 8 9

ISBN 1 84417 211 2
Catalogue No. 1500689

Edited by Graham Harris
Cover design by Angela Selfe
Artwork by Helen Gannon
Typesetting by Richard Weaver

Printed and bound in Great Britain

Contents

About the author

Chris Stafford first became involved in working with young people at the St John's Harborne (Birmingham) Easter event – a week-long youth event where teams took assemblies in local schools, followed by after-school activities at the church. During his ordination training at St John's College, Nottingham, he was a member of the schools assembly and drama teams, and also developed an interest in puppetry, tricks and visual aids.

Chris was ordained in 1999 and now works in the Diocese of Liverpool. His first appointment was as curate at St Philip's Church, Westbrook, Warrington. Most of the assembly outlines appearing in this book were tried and tested at St Philip's C of E school.

Introduction

Off the Peg Assemblies is a collection of 30 assemblies for KS1 and KS2. They are ready to use, divided into four distinct sections:

- Biblical characters
- The life of Christ/the Christian life
- The Lord's Prayer
- Environment

The outlines can be used word for word, but I would encourage users to enjoy developing the ideas and experimenting with the concepts, as I have done. I hope the outlines will be used like a child with a dressing-up box – mixing the items to create something new, relevant and exciting!

Reverend Doctor Chris Stafford

Jacob's ladder

Preparation

During the assembly you will make a paper ladder, using the diagram on page 9 as your guide.

The more paper you use the higher the ladder will go, but you will need strong hands and good scissors to cut through a lot of paper. It might be better to start the assembly with the paper roll fastened with sticky tape, ready to cut. As an optional extra you could always make angel figures to add to the ladder in the assembly.

Themes

Jacob's dream
God's love for us
Being special

Bible reference

Genesis 28:10-22

Bible story

Things were not good for Jacob. He had made his big brother, Esau, really angry. Jacob felt sick – he was sorry for what he'd done. He was ashamed, but he was also very worried. He wanted to stay at home but it was too risky, because Esau was after him – big time. Jacob felt that the safest thing to do was to run away from home – at least until his brother had calmed down. Jacob decided to set off to see his uncle Laban. But the journey to Laban's house was long and hard. There were no roads and he had to cross the hot, dry desert all alone.

It started to get dark as he crossed the desert. He could no longer see to walk, so he decided to get some sleep. He picked up a large stone to use under his head for a pillow, and he lay down on the desert floor.

It wasn't long before Jacob was asleep, and he began to dream. It was unlike any dream he'd ever had. What did he dream about?

Now introduce your ladder. Cut or tear the sheets of paper as shown. Once you have extended your ladder continue with the story.

In his dream Jacob saw a ladder. It was so big that it stood on the ground and went right up into the sky. Angels flew up and down it. From heaven Jacob heard a voice saying: 'I am God. I will be with you. I will keep you safe. One day you will return to this land with all your family. That's a promise.'

Jacob woke up. He was shocked by the power of his dream. He thought: 'Why should God want to talk to me here in the middle of a desert, of all places? I thought you only found God in special places.'

Even more amazing was the fact that God wanted to talk to *him*, especially after he had been so horrible to his brother. He was flabbergasted.

'I thought I was a nobody,' he said. 'I thought I was alone . . . a runaway . . . unimportant. But I must be *somebody* because God came to speak to *me*! I must be important to him because he made a promise to be with me. Jacob thought: 'I want to remember this spot forever.'

So, early the next morning he picked up his stone pillow. He collected more stones and made a big pile, so that it looked like a pillar. He used them to mark the place where he'd had the dream. And he gave the place a special name. He called it Bethel because he'd met God there.

Application Jacob was in a real mess. In time, things did work out for him, but today we're just thinking about him while he was on his journey. Jacob learnt an important lesson in the desert.

Emphasise the fact that in the story a *non-place* becomes a special place (by the fact that it is given a name), and a *nobody* realises that they are *somebody*, by the fact that God comes to talk to them. Jacob realises that he is not a *nobody*, but is special and unique. He has a place in God's plans.

At times we may feel like Jacob. We may not feel special – in fact we may feel quite ordinary. We might not live in a grand house or a palace, where important people live. But God wants us to see that wherever we live, whoever we are – we are all unique and special to God. Everybody is somebody to God, and he has a good plan for each of us.

Think about those things during the day.

Closing prayer *Dear God,*

Thank you for the story of Jacob. At times we think we're nobody special – ordinary and unimportant. Help us always to remember that we are special and important to you.

Amen.

Suggested songs Father God I wonder (*Kidsource*)
God is good (*Kidsource, Junior Praise*)
God knows me (*BBC Come and Praise 1*)
God loves you (*Kidsource*)
Have you seen the pussycat? (*Kidsource, Junior Praise*)
I'm special (*Kidsource, Junior Praise*)
My Jesus, my Saviour (*Kidsource*)
We are climbing (*BBC Come and Praise 1*)

Jacob's ladder

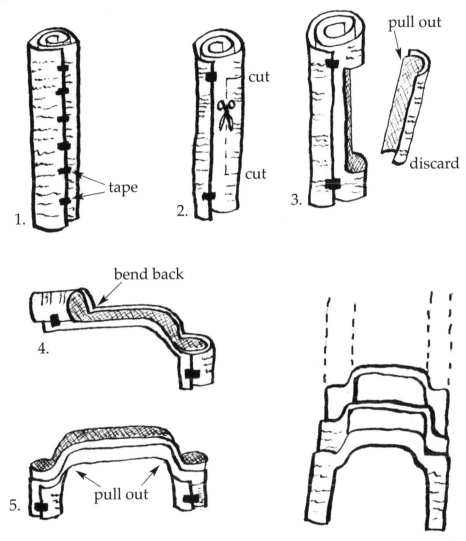

Roll up several sheets of newspaper and tape as shown. Cut out piece as shown. Bend roll back to make bridge shape. Gently pull out insides from each side to make ladder.

Joseph and his jealous brothers

Preparation

Place pictures of sheep around the room – easily visible to the children.

Start the assembly with two characters in conflict with each other. You could use puppets made from simple materials (e.g. socks or paper plates) or children could mime the actions as you narrate.

Themes

Story of Joseph
Highlights family conflict and forgiveness

Bible reference

Genesis 37-45

Narrator:

'Here's Oliver. Oliver, I have a present for you. (*Pause and mime presentation*) Yes, it is a lovely scarf, isn't it? Long, and very beautiful. Well, I shouldn't really say so, but since you ask, yes, it was very expensive. You look very pleased with it, Oliver. Yes, you can wear it all the time. (*Addressing children*) But there's a problem. How can Oliver run in it and keep the sheep together? (*Pointing to all the sheep round the room*) . . . He'll trip over! I tell you what, Oliver. You no longer have to work hard all day. You can stay at home, watch television, have friends round and play games.'

(*Oliver looks very pleased at this news*)

Narrator:

'Ooh, here comes Rachael. She'll have to be responsible for looking after all the sheep. Hmmm . . . she doesn't look very pleased about that, does she? What's that, Rachael . . . why isn't Oliver helping to look after the sheep? Well, I've sent him home. I said he could stay there while you look after the sheep. What's that? You can't. (*Turn to the children*) Rachael says she can't look after all the sheep. (*Calling out*) Oh yes you can! (*Get the children to join in*). Anyway, why can't you? It's not fair, you say?

Rachael says it reminds her of a story in the Bible about a man called Joseph.

Well, I know the one you mean, so let me tell it and then we can all see who's being unfair.'

Bible story *This story has been written for audience participation – encourage the children to make the following responses when you say the relevant word (you can speed up towards the end for dramatic effect):*

Joseph – *bow*

Coat – shout: '*it's not fair!*'

Egypt – *make a pyramid shape with your arms*

Joseph (*bow*) had a new **coat** ('*it's not fair!*'). His dad had given it to him. It was a special **coat** ('*it's not fair!*') . . . not one that you would work in. And **Joseph** (*bow*) wore it all the time.

'Look at me,' **Joseph** (*bow*) said to his brothers. 'Look at me in my new **coat**.' (*it's not fair!*).

'It's not fair,' his brothers shouted. 'Dad's always giving you things. None of us has a new **coat**!' ('*it's not fair!*') . . . and they were jealous.

Joseph (*bow*) would tell his dad tales about his brothers whenever they got into mischief, making them cross. Then he started to tell them his dreams: 'We cut the corn in the fields and tied it into bundles,' **Joseph** (*bow*) said. 'And your bundles bowed down to mine.'

'I had another dream. In this one the sun, the moon and 11 stars all bowed down to me, **Joseph**.' (*bow*)

Aarrrgh! This made them so angry. Who does he think he is?

One day, when his brothers were in the fields looking after the sheep, **Joseph**'s (*bow*) dad said to **Joseph**: (*bow*) 'Go to your brothers and make sure everything is all right.'

So **Joseph** (*bow*) set off wearing his new **coat** ('*it's not fair!*'). The brothers saw him and his **coat** ('*it's not fair!*') in the distance and said: 'Look at that dreamer. Let's get rid of him.'

So, when **Joseph** (*bow*) reached them, they ripped off his **coat** ('*it's not fair!*') and thought about killing him. Now at about that time some men came riding by, heading for **Egypt** (*pyramid shape*). 'Let them have **Joseph**,' (*bow*) one of them suggested. So **Joseph** (*bow*) was sold as a slave to travellers, and taken to far-away **Egypt** (*pyramid shape*).

As they walked back home, they thought about what they would tell their dad. 'Let's say that fierce, wild animals have killed him,' one said, and they made **Joseph**'s (*bow*) **coat** (*it's not fair!*) all dirty and messy . . . so that their dad would believe their story.

But God had a special plan for **Joseph** (*bow*). **Joseph** (*bow*) was clever, and in time, he did become important. In fact he became the most important man in **Egypt** (*pyramid shape*), after the king, of course.

Joseph (*bow*) had the job of ensuring that there was enough food in the land. God had told him that there would be seven years when there would be plenty of food, followed by seven bad years.

In the good years, **Joseph** (*bow*) stored some food ready, so that no one would go hungry when the bad years came.

But **Joseph**'s (*bow*) family, back home, had nothing left to eat.

'You must go to **Egypt** (*pyramid shape*) to buy food,' **Joseph**'s (*bow*) dad said to the brothers. 'I've heard there is food there.'

It was a long journey, but they had to go.

As they walked, they thought about **Joseph** (*bow*) and his **coat** ('*it's not fair!*'), and they wished they hadn't been so cruel.

When the brothers arrived, they bowed in front of **Joseph**, (*bow*) but they didn't know it was him. **Joseph** (*bow*) burst into tears.

'It's me . . . **Joseph**,' (*bow*) he said.

'We're in trouble now,' his brothers thought.

But **Joseph** (*bow*) simply hugged them and forgave them. And he asked them to come and live with him in **Egypt** (*pyramid shape*).

Application   That's the end of the story about people falling out with each other.

Suggest that the children think about who was right and who was wrong. In families people will fall out with each other at times. The important thing is that people should be prepared to forgive, as Joseph forgave his brothers. Saying sorry or forgiving someone is not always easy. Ask the children to put themselves in the shoes of Joseph. What would they have done? Would they have forgiven their brothers and cared for them now they were in need of food? Or would they send them away empty-handed?

Take suggestions from the children

Point out that the ending would have been different if Joseph hadn't forgiven them. Read out Genesis 45:5-8, as you talk about Joseph's forgiving attitude.

Closing prayer

Dear God,

We thank you God, for the way in which Joseph took care of his family in Egypt, when they came to him for food. Help us to be thoughtful and kind, and to act in ways that Jesus would want us to.

Amen.

End by reminding the children about the volunteers/puppets who helped you at the start. Say that they also had a falling out and that we can sometimes be in similar situations. Perhaps we can forgive each other and make a new start?

Suggested songs

Bind us together Lord (*Junior Praise*)
God forgave my sin (*Junior Praise*)
Have you heard? (*Kidsource*)
In our work and in our play (*Junior Praise*)
Make me a channel (*Kidsource*)
O Lord, all the world belongs to you (*BBC Come and Praise 1*)
One more step (*Junior Praise, BBC Come and Praise 1*)
Peace I give to you (*Junior Praise*)
Spirit of God (*BBC Come and Praise 1*)

Moses and the best way to live

Preparation Copy the snakes and ladders game (on page 17) onto an overhead projector acetate. You will also need two playing pieces (which can be distinguished by the shadow they create on the screen), a large dice, and a whistle.

Themes
| The Ten Commandments
| Rules for living and school rules

Bible reference
| Exodus 20:1-17

Bible story Ask for two volunteers to play snakes and ladders. Once they have had two or three turns each, blow the whistle and tell them that there are now no rules. The children will probably look confused but carry on playing as before. As they do so, interrupt them periodically with the whistle and explain that a) they shouldn't move as per the number on the dice, b) they shouldn't take it in turns, c) they shouldn't go up the ladders and down the snakes, as these are all rules. Even if one reaches the end there is now no rule to say that they have won! You might even find that the children gave up playing because there was simply no point in continuing.

Explain that it is very hard to play a game without any rules – you simply don't know what you should or shouldn't do.

Another game will help to make the point. This one is based on *Simon says*, which all the children can play, although you may wish to substitute *The Head Teacher says* for *Simon says*! Once the children have responded appropriately to a few statements, again tell them that there are no rules. If children follow the instructions tell them they are out, because you're not playing by the rules.

Emphasise how hard it is without rules. Without them people are at a loss. We need rules to play a game. We also need rules to live by. We need to know what is expected of us. We need to know what we can and can't do.

Refer to some rules in school such as:
- don't run in the corridor;

- don't talk while the teacher is speaking;
- show respect for one another, etc.

Rules make life easier. What would happen if the school had no rules? (*Respond to any suggestions*) Rules help us to live, to work, and to play together. If we follow the rules, the school will run more smoothly.

Now tell the story of Moses. If necessary, briefly summarise the events of the Exodus by telling them that many years ago, God's people were in a bad way. They were living in a country called Egypt, but they weren't happy because they had been made into slaves. They were cruelly beaten by men with whips, and were forced to work hard.

But God chose a man called Moses to help rescue them. God chose Moses to rescue the people and lead them out of Egypt to a new place – a new land.

Why did God do this? He wanted his people to be free. He didn't want them to be slaves. So he led them to a new land where they could live. He also gave them some rules to live by. Tell the children that God gave his people ten rules. Here are five of them, using the hand as a visual aid to aid memory:

Thumb:

Ask a child to pick up a piece of paper or another item without using their thumb. This will be very difficult to do. The thumb is very important and without it we can do very little. In fact, you could say it's the most important finger. God said to his people: 'Always remember that I am important. Out of all the things that you have, don't let anything else take my place.'

First finger:

The 'pointing finger'. We use it when we point at something and say: 'I want one of those. I want a computer like hers; I want some trainers like his.' God said: 'Don't be greedy for what other people have.'

Middle finger:

Is the longest, the *tallest* of all. Sometimes, if someone catches you lying, they might say: 'Don't tell tall stories.' And so the tall finger reminds us not to tell tall stories or lies. God said: 'Don't tell lies.'

Ring finger:

People who are married often wear a ring on this finger. It's a sign that a man and a woman love each other. God said: 'I want those people to keep their special love for each other.' When a man and a woman love each other they sometimes have children, which leads us to . . .

Little finger:

Baby finger. It's the smallest finger. It's small compared to the ring finger. And so it reminds us all to look up to our parents – to listen to them and to make them pleased about our behaviour.

So, those are five of the ten rules God gave his people.

Remind the children that God rescued his people. He took them to a new land. He showed them *where* to live and he showed them *how* to live. The rules were given to help the people live together. God was showing them the way to live properly.

Encourage the children to reflect on the rules during the day. Of course, the people of God didn't always keep those rules, and neither do we. We sometimes tell lies, we are sometimes greedy and we don't always see God as being important. But in giving the rules, God was showing us how to live together.

In a moment of quiet ask the children to reflect on the rules. Is there one rule in particular that God is speaking to them about? Ask them to go on thinking about the rules during the day as they look at their hands.

Closing prayer

Dear God,

Thank you, Lord, that you give us rules to live by. Help us to follow them, so that we may work and live together in peace and happiness.

Amen.

Suggested songs

Abba Father (*Junior Praise*)
In days of old (*Kidsource*)
In our work and in our play (*Junior Praise*)
I want to walk with Jesus Christ (*Junior Praise*)
Lord Jesus Christ (*Junior Praise*)
One more step (*Junior Praise, BBC Come and Praise 1*)
Spirit of peace (*BBC Come and Praise 2*)
Uh well, it's excellent to be obedient (*Kidsource*)

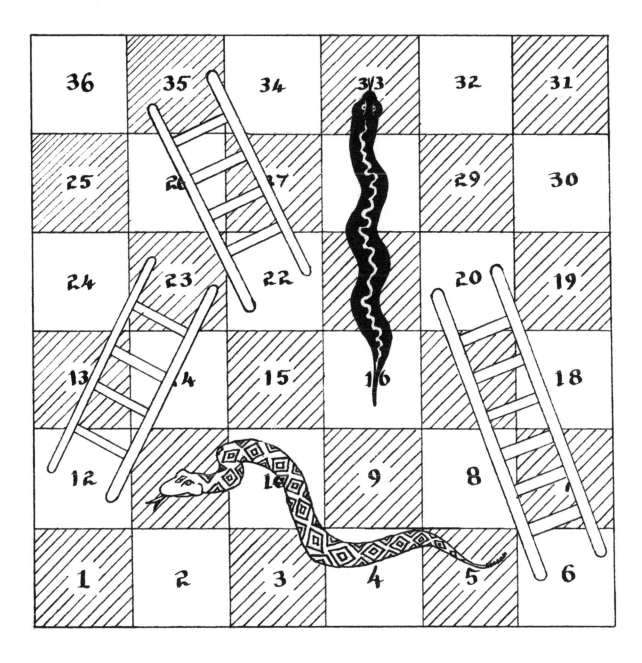

David and Goliath

Preparation

There are various props you can introduce into this assembly. For the way in you will need a packet of balloons and a straight piece of wire about 60cm long. Metal coat hangers are ideal for this. Simply use the flat bottom part of the hanger with one of the sides. Cut the wire with a hacksaw, straighten the wire as much as possible, and file one end to a sharp point (*to avoid accidental injury on the point, place the tip in some modelling clay or a bottle cork until ready for use*).

For the postcard trick, you will need to prepare a postcard as shown in the diagram on page 21.

You may like to create your own Goliath! If possible, borrow a tall step ladder from the school. Cover it with a couple of large sheets (*peg the sheets together at the back*) and make a large, fierce face for the top.

Themes
- Feeling helpless
- Strength in weakness
- Determination
- Finding a way forward

Bible reference
- 1 Samuel 17:1-54

Bible story

As an introduction, talk about things that are seemingly impossible. For example ask if it is possible to stick a pin into an ordinary balloon without it bursting? Stick your large pin into one of the inflated balloons and allow it to burst.

Now ask if it is possible to walk through a postcard? Invite a child out to try.

Tell the children that sometimes we can feel really helpless. When we hear the news on television, we feel unable to do anything about the wars, about the lack of food in some countries, and about the damage being done to the environment. What can we do that will change the situation?

Sometimes we are so sure that we can't do anything to change those situations, so we don't even try. Perhaps refer to the child and the postcard – did they actually try to walk through it?

Say to the children that you are going to tell them a story about a group of people who felt so sure they couldn't do anything about a situation they didn't even try.

Ask the children if anyone *knows* how tall they are? (*Take answers*)

Now introduce them to Goliath (*point to your ladder with the face*). Goliath was simply enormous. He was almost three metres tall, and he was like an iron man. He was much stronger than anyone else – no one could hurt him. His armour weighed 55 kilograms (you might like to show them how much this is in bags of sugar!). Explain how you feel quite scared just standing there next to him!

Goliath had lots of horrible friends. They were called *the People from the Sea*. They had picked a fight with the people of Israel. They wanted to push them off the land and take it all for themselves.

The people who lived in Israel saw Goliath and they were terrified! They didn't know what to do. To make matters worse, Goliath would tease them and make fun of them. He would stand in front of them saying: 'I dare anyone to fight me . . . and when I win, you will be our slaves forever!'

But no one wanted to fight him. They all stood there shaking with fear. Oh dear! Against Goliath they all felt rather small. What *could* they do, he was *so* big?

It just so happened that a few miles away, there was a young boy called David. David was a shepherd – he looked after sheep. He would keep a careful eye on them and he would keep them safe. David was good at his job.

Now David's brothers were among the soldiers of Israel. One day David's dad called him, and said: 'Go and see how your brothers are. And take this bread, they may be hungry.'

So David got to see the army. He saw his brothers. He also saw Goliath standing there, shouting: 'Well, what are you people waiting for? Send someone to come and fight me. If you dare…'

David also got to see how afraid all the soldiers were. He said: 'We shouldn't let someone push us around like that, even if he is very big. Who does he think he is?'

David made such a fuss the king sent for him. 'I'm not scared,' said David. 'You are only a boy,' said the king. 'How can you fight Goliath?'

David said: 'Look, I've kept my dad's sheep safe from lions and bears. Why should this Goliath be any different? And, anyway, God will help me.'

The king admired David's boldness, so he gave David his own armour to wear. He gave him a big helmet and long sword. But David just looked silly. They were far too big and heavy – he couldn't even move! 'I'm not used to fighting with armour,' he said. 'I'm used to fighting wild animals with my sling and stick.'

So David went down to the stream and chose five smooth stones for his sling. Then he went to find the giant. When Goliath saw David he went berserk. 'What's *this*? You're sending a boy with a stick. Do I look like a dog?'

David answered: 'You come to me with a sword and spear. But I come to you in the name of God.' The giant ran forwards to fight David. David put a stone in his sling, whirled it round, and let go. Whack! It hit Goliath straight between the eyes and he fell to the ground.

When the Philistine gang saw this they thought, if one small boy can do this, what can a whole army do? And they turned and ran.

Application   The soldiers were so sure they couldn't win against Goliath they didn't even try. As far as they were concerned it was no use trying.

Now take another inflated balloon. This time, make sure that you put the wire pin on the nipple (opposite the knot). The balloon is thicker here and should allow you to push the pin right through without bursting. Practise beforehand, and if you want to give the balloon even more strength you can add a piece of clear sticking tape to the area where the pin will enter and exit the balloon. Keep pushing the pin through – making sure that it exits by the knot (again where the balloon is thicker) or where you have placed some clear sticking tape.

For the postcard, invite your volunteer out again. This time present the cut postcard. It should fold out sufficiently for them to walk through!

Sometimes we may feel like those soldiers in the army. Sometimes we may think: 'There's no point in trying. I know it can't be done. I know I can't do it.' David was willing to have a go and he succeeded. Comment that even if we can't see a way to do it, that doesn't mean it can't be done. Sometimes we need help from other people, such as our teachers at school, but together we can often find a way forward and solve a problem. You could also make the point this might make some children think of bullies they know. You can explain that even though those who are being bullied may feel helpless with no way out, there is a way forward if they talk to their teacher or parent.

Closing prayer   *Father God,*

We thank you that you love us and care for us.

Like the soldiers in our story, sometimes we feel small and helpless. Sometimes we feel that there is no point in trying. Help us to remember that you are always with us. Help us to remember that with you and each other, we can find answers to those things that trouble us.

Help us to work with you to make this world a better place for us all to live.

Amen.

Suggested songs
Be bold (*Junior Praise*)
Father, I place into your hands (*Junior Praise*)
Give us hope (*BBC Come and Praise 2*)
Have you heard (*Kidsource*)
One more step (*Junior Praise, Kidsource, BBC Come and Praise 1*)
Spirit of peace (*BBC Come and Praise 2*)
Whenever I'm afraid (*Kidsource*)

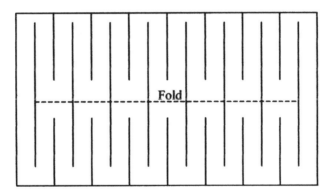

You will need a postcard of approx. 10cm by 15cm. Mark the postcard with the lines as shown above, then fold the card in half lengthways. With the card folded, make cuts from the fold *almost* to the edges. Keeping the card folded make the second set of cuts from the edges almost to the fold. Open the card and make the final cut along the fold itself – but don't cut through to the outside edges (only as far as the dotted line)! The card is now ready to walk through!

Nehemiah's prayer

Preparation

This assembly is designed to involve all the children. In advance make a tin-can telephone. Choose two tins that are not too deep, clean and with their lids completely removed. Make sure that there are no sharp edges. Make a hole in the centre of the base of each tin, using hammer and nail. Thread a length of thin string (up to 10 metres long) through the holes, and tie knots on the inside of each tin. The phone is now ready to use.

Themes

Nehemiah
God hears our prayer
Coping with difficulties
Determination

Bible references

Nehemiah 1:1-11 and Chapter 2
Psalm 116:1
Luke 11:1-13

Nehemiah
Who, me?

King
Pom pom-pom pom

Prayed
Hands together

Sad
Ah

Jerusalem
Bow

Happy
Hooray

Army
Tramp tramp

Sanballat
Boo

Have a short practice before you start.

Bible story

There was once a young man called **Nehemiah** (*who, me?*). Yes. And **Nehemiah** (*who, me?*) – oh yes – worked in Babylon for the **king** (*pom pom-pom pom*). And **Nehemiah** (*who, me?*) – that's the one – became so important, he worked as a wine taster; tasting wine for the **king** (*pom pom-pom pom*) to make sure that it was safe to drink.

One day, while **Nehemiah** (*who, me?*) was working in the palace, he heard all about the state of **Jerusalem** (*bow*). For several days he looked very **sad** (*ah*), for **Jerusalem** (*bow*) was his home. So he **prayed** (*hands together*) to God. He said: 'Sorry,' and he **prayed** (*hands together*) for help.

When the **king** (*pom pom-pom pom*), saw **Nehemiah** (*who, me?*) he asked 'Why are you so sad (*aah*), **Nehemiah**? (*who, me?*) 'Yes you,' said the **king** (*pom pom-pom pom*).

Nehemiah (*who, me?*) said, 'How can I help looking **sad** (*ah*), because **Jerusalem** (*bow*) is in such a mess. The old city is in ruins.'

The **king** (*pom pom-pom pom*) replied, 'What is it you want?' **Nehemiah** (*who, me?*) **prayed** (*hands together*) to God, and then he said, 'If the **king** (*pom pom-pom pom*) is pleased with me, let me go to **Jerusalem** (*bow*) so that I can rebuild it.'

He was **happy** (*hooray*) for him to go. He gave **Nehemiah** (*who, me?*) a letter for the keeper of the royal forest, so that he could take wood for rebuilding **Jerusalem** (*bow*). The **king** (*pom pom-pom pom*) gave him all he asked for, because God was with him.

So, the royal **army** (*tramp tramp*), with **Nehemiah** (*who, me?*) left Babylon for **Jerusalem** (*bow*). In the middle of the night, **Nehemiah** (*who, me?*) got up, and with a few men from the **army** (*tramp tramp*), walked round **Jerusalem** (*bow*) and looked at the broken walls. In the morning, he spoke to the Jewish people. He said, 'This is a **sad** (*ah*), sight. Let's rebuild these walls and make God **happy** (*hooray*). And he told them how God had been with him, and what the **king** (*pom pom-pom pom*) had said to him.

Now **Sanballat** (*boo*) didn't like **Nehemiah** (*who, me?*). He had no time for **Jerusalem** (*bow*) or the Jewish people. So when he heard this, he became very angry. **Sanballat** (*boo*) tried to stop them, by stirring up trouble. But **Nehemiah** (*who, me?*) **prayed** (*hands together*) regularly. And with God's help rebuilt **Jerusalem** (*bow*) so that the people were safe and **happy** (*hooray*).

Application Explain that the story about Nehemiah takes place many years ago. God's people had been living in Israel (the Promised Land), when they were attacked and invaded by people from Babylon. Their city of Jerusalem was trashed.

Nehemiah was one of the lucky ones. Not only did he survive; he had become an important servant to the king and queen of Babylon. But he was worried about the state of Jerusalem.

When the king noticed his sadness, he used that opportunity. What did he do first?

Take suggestions from the children. Before telling the king what he wanted, he prayed.

Nehemiah investigated the ruin of Jerusalem by night, a bit like a spy. This was because he knew he had enemies, and as soon as he started to rebuild, he attracted the attention of Sanballat. Sanballat caused Nehemiah endless trouble. Finish by talking about Nehemiah's response to the trouble. He did not give up. He prayed about his situation and knew that God was with him. With God's help, the work of rebuilding was finished.

Encourage the children to think some more about prayer. Tell them that you have brought in your mobile telephone (you might tease them a little before showing them the phone, e.g. tell them that it never needs to be charged up, it works any time and anywhere, and every call is free!). Now bring out the phone and ask for two volunteers. Ask the children to walk apart until the string is tight (*the string must be tight for this to work*). Now ask one of the children to talk whilst the other listens.

Prayer is a little bit like having a mobile telephone – a direct line to God! Wherever we are, whatever the time of day, we can pray to God and he will hear us and help us.

Closing prayer Ask the children to repeat each line of the prayer:

With thanks we pray to you, O God.
For trust we pray to you, O God.
For strength we pray to you, O God.
For health we pray to you, O God.

Amen.

Suggested songs Abba Father (*Junior Praise, Kidsource*)
Be bold, be strong (*Junior Praise, Kidsource*)
Father, hear the prayer we offer (*BBC Come and Praise 1, Junior Praise*)
F-U-N-E-N-R-G? (*Kidsource*)
Lord Jesus Christ (*Junior Praise*)
Lord of all hopefulness (*BBC Come and Praise 1, Junior Praise*)
My God is so big (*Junior Praise, Kidsource*)
Seek ye first the kingdom of God (*Junior Praise, Kidsource*)
The Lord's Prayer (*Junior Praise, BBC Come and Praise 1*)
When the road is rough and steep (*Junior Praise*)

Jonah's whale of a tale

Preparation
This story has been written for maximum participation – the children are encouraged to make responses to key words, as follows:

Jonah – *not me!*
Go – *point with one hand*
Ran – *puff puff*
Sea – *splish splash*
Storm – *make waves with your arms*
Tired – *yawn*
Shout – *help!*

You could print the above key words on strips of paper and get volunteers to hold them at the front. You may also like to add sound effects if you have access to a sound-effects CD.

For the Application section you will need two paper bags (of the same size and colour), some confetti or bits of coloured paper, and a plain A5 sheet of paper. Cut the top off the first paper bag and make two or three holes in the bottom (see diagram on page 28). Put the confetti into the second paper bag, and glue the first bag inside the second (glue along the edge of the first bag round the top). You should find that the second bag is barely visible, with confetti trapped in the lining. During the application, bursting the bag will release the confetti (but keep the scrunched up paper in bag 1 hidden).

Bible story
One day God said: 'I've got a job for you **Jonah** (*not me!*). Yes, you! **Go** (*point*) to Nineveh. The people there are doing bad things. I want you to tell them to stop.'

Jonah (*not me!*) didn't want to do it. 'Not me!' he said, and he **ran** (*puff puff*) away from God. He **ran** (*puff puff*) away to the **sea** (*splish splash*).

He didn't like the people of Nineveh. He wanted God to hate them too. 'If I **go** (*point*) to warn them,' he said to himself, 'they might change, and God might be happy with them.' **Jonah** (*not me!*) didn't want that – so he **ran** (*puff puff*) away.

Jonah (*not me!*) **ran** (*puff puff*) to the **sea** (*splish splash*) and caught a ship going the other way. He was so **tired** (*yawn*) he fell asleep. He was so **tired** (*yawn*) he didn't hear the wind blow, louder and louder. He didn't feel the waves rock the boat. He was so **tired** (*yawn*) he didn't even hear the sailors' **shout** (*help!*). **Jonah** (*not me!*) didn't know there was a **storm** (*make wave*) . . . a frightening **storm** (*make wave*).

'Wake up!' said the captain, giving **Jonah** (*not me!*) a hard shake.

'Go (*point*) and say your prayers. **Shout** (*help!*) to God to save us.'

But **Jonah** (*not me!*) **ran** (*puff puff*) away from God. How could he **go** (*point*) to God and **shout** (*help!*)?

'This **storm** (*make wave*) is because of me,' he said. 'You must throw me into the **sea** (*splish splash*).'

'We can't do that,' the sailors replied.

'But if you don't,' he said, 'the **storm** (*make wave*) will sink the boat. And you will all be drowned.'

So they did. And the **storm** (*make wave*) stopped.

Jonah (*not me!*) sank, down, down, down beneath the waves. But God heard **Jonah** (*not me!*) **shout** (*help!*), and he sent a huge fish and . . .

Gobble! What strange sounds! **Jonah** (*not me!*) was inside the fish, but he was safe. It was dark and full of slippery, slimy **sea** (*splish splash*) . . . weed!

'God,' he said, 'I **shout** (*help!*) and you save me. Thank you. I'm sorry I **ran** (*puff puff*) away.'

'If I ever get out of this fish I'll do as you tell me.'

Jonah (*not me!*) was stuck inside the fish for three days. Then . . .

Burp! . . . the fish spat **Jonah** (*not me!*) out onto dry land.

Then God said, '**Go** (*point*) to Nineveh.' This time he **ran** (*puff puff*) to Nineveh to tell the people, 'God is cross with you for what you are doing.'

The people of Nineveh were sorry. There was a loud **shout** (*help!*) to God, as they decided to change their ways and stop being nasty – and God was kind to them.

Jonah (*not me!*) sat in the hot sun. He was **tired** (*yawn*) and very cross! 'I knew this would happen,' he grumbled. 'I just knew it. I wanted you to punish those people. But you've been nice to them!'

But God said: 'Think of all those people: men, women and children. I love everyone – yes, even the people of Nineveh. Isn't that a good thing?'

Application

The people of Nineveh changed. They saw the wrong they had been doing. They said sorry and God forgave them. They changed their ways and had a fresh start.

It took Jonah a bit longer to change. He kept running away from God, hoping that everything would be OK. It was only when he was in a real mess that he finally said sorry, and did as God wanted. Explain to the children that saying sorry isn't always easy, and we can try to put it off.

To help the children think about forgiveness and change a little more, bring out your paper bag. Show the children that the bag is empty. Now take the A5 sheet of paper, and write some words on it that describe how the people of Nineveh felt (e.g. hate, anger, nasty). Put the paper into the bag. Say that the people of Nineveh were sorry and God forgave them. They changed their ways, and stopped being nasty, as God wanted. So the people had a fresh start. Blow up the bag and burst it – the paper has changed. The nasty words have disappeared; we now have colourful paper (the confetti). What a difference saying sorry can make to our lives!

Reflection

Who will you be like? Will you be like Jonah, who took a long time to say sorry and got himself into a real mess? Or will you be like the people of Nineveh, who said sorry quickly, and had a fresh start. Encourage the children to say sorry to anyone they need to, and to have a fresh start.

Closing prayer

Dear God,

Thank you for the story of Jonah and the people of Nineveh. Help *us* to be ready to say sorry, and to admit the mistakes we make. Help us to remember that if we say sorry, we can be forgiven and can make a fresh start.

Amen.

Suggested songs

Colours of day (*Junior Praise, BBC Come and Praise 1*)
Come, listen to my tale (*Junior Praise*)
God forgave my sin (*Junior Praise*)
Make me a channel (*Kidsource, Junior Praise, BBC Come and Praise 2*)
O sinner man (*Junior Praise*)
One more step (*Junior Praise, BBC Come and Praise 1*)
Spirit of God (*BBC Come and Praise 1*)
What a whale of a tale (*Kidsource*)
We are climbing (*BBC Come and Praise 1*)

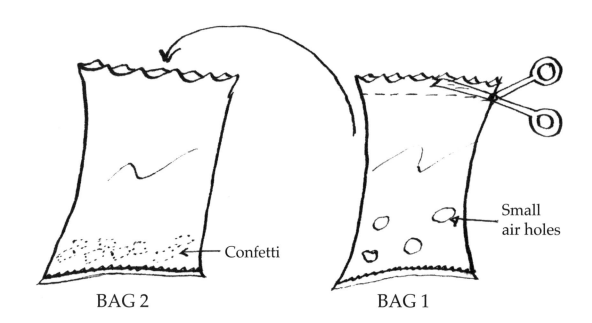

BAG 2

Confetti

BAG 1

Small air holes

The call of Peter

Preparation

For the fishing game you will need: a whistle, two dozen paper fish (use a simple fish shape about 10cm across, each with a paper-clip attached) two empty baskets, a tray, two rods with string and magnets attached.

For the magic tubes you will need: a plastic cup, a paper-clip, two pieces of coloured card about 30cm square, a mug filled with confetti and a jug of water. Twist the paper-clip open to form a hook (an 'S' shape). Stick the paper-clip to the outside of the cup. Now take one sheet of card and use it to form a tube, by wrapping it around the outside of the cup. Tape the card to keep it in a tube shape. Repeat with the second piece of card – only make this tube slightly wider than the first (the first tube should be able to slide freely inside the second tube). Hook the bent clip on both tubes, so that the cup hangs inside (see diagram, page 31).

> **Themes**
> | Call of Peter
> | Following God
> | Trust
>
> **Bible references**
> | Matthew 4:18-22
> | Mark 1:16-20
> | Luke 5:1-11

Bible story

Use the fishing game as a way in. Ask for two volunteers. Place the tray with paper fish between them. Explain that they are going fishing . . . but that they have just 30 seconds to catch as many fish as they can! Fish caught are placed in one of the baskets. Blow the whistle when the time is up. You may like to compare the results!

Tell the children that the story is all about fishing. One day Jesus was walking beside Lake Galilee, when he saw boats pulled up on the beach. The fishermen had left them and were washing their nets.

Jesus climbed into one of the boats. It belonged to a man called Peter. 'Peter', Jesus asked, 'will you push the boat out a little from the shore?'

Jesus sat in the boat and spoke to a large crowd that had gathered.

When Jesus had finished talking, he said to Peter, 'Let's go out further to deeper water, and you and your friends can catch some fish.'

'But Jesus,' said Peter, 'we've worked all through the night and didn't catch a thing. And what's more, we're tired . . . we're shattered. But if you say so, we will.'

So they went out into deeper water and let down their nets.

Encourage the children to think about Peter. What was he thinking? Perhaps he wondered if it was all a waste of time. After all, what did Jesus know about fishing?

Peter tried to pull his net up into the boat. 'Oh no,' he thought. 'Now it's got caught on a rock at the bottom of the lake. No, wait. The net moved. This is a big catch!' And he caught so many fish in his net he had to shout to the shore for help from another boat . . . but even then, both boats were so full of fish that they nearly sank!

When Peter saw this, he fell at Jesus' knees. Peter had been a fisherman all his life, and he knew that this was no ordinary catch – this was a miracle. Jesus had done something special.

'Come with me,' said Jesus. 'Don't be afraid. Come and catch bigger fish.' Jesus didn't mean the fish in the lake . . . he was talking about *people*! He wanted Peter to help him tell everyone about God's plans for them.

Peter pulled his boat up onto the beach, left his nets, and followed Jesus. Peter was one of the first special friends of Jesus.

Application   Encourage the children to think about the story a little more with the tubes (diagram, page 31). Ask the children if they trust you.

Having assembled the two tubes and the plastic cup, slide the outside tube from the bottom downwards, making sure that the hidden cup stays in place. Hold the outside tube up so that the children can see it is empty. Replace, sliding it from the bottom up. Now remove the inside tube, again sliding it out from the bottom downwards, keeping the cup in place. Show them that this tube is also empty (remember to keep the cup hidden from the children the whole time).

Now place both tubes over the mug. Pour some water from the jug into the tubes. The children will think the water has gone into the mug, when in reality it is in your hidden plastic cup. Ask the children again if they trust you.

Now throw the contents of the mug at the kids. To their surprise, confetti and not water comes out.

Explain that if we are going to follow Jesus, we need to trust him. If we're going to move forward and grow in our faith, then we need to trust God for all the good things that he has for us.

Remind the children about Peter. He left the greatest catch of his life. Why? Because it showed him something about Jesus: he realised that Jesus could be trusted. Peter was feeling tired, he'd worked hard all night. Night was the best time to go fishing. He'd been fishing at the best possible time and hadn't caught a thing. What was the use of trying in the daytime, when it was light?

But when Jesus asked him to throw his nets out again for another try, he didn't say, 'Don't be daft – you know nothing about fishing!' He simply did it. And it was the biggest catch ever!

Peter learnt that day that he could trust Jesus. Even when things didn't seem to be in his favour, he still trusted Jesus. We can trust Jesus too, for he cares for us and wants the best for us.

Closing prayer *Dear God,*

In your love, you have called us, like Peter, to know you. Please help us to trust you, for you only want the best for us. Help us to know you more clearly, to follow you more nearly and to love you more dearly, day by day.

Amen.

Suggested songs A man for all the people (*BBC Come and Praise 1*)
Big man (*Junior Praise*)
Colours of day (*Junior Praise, BBC Come and Praise 1*)
I danced in the morning (*Junior Praise, BBC Come and Praise 1*)
It's an adventure (*Kidsource*)
Jesus wants me (*Kidsource*)
One more step (*Junior Praise, BBC Come and Praise 1*)
Spirit of God (*BBC Come and Praise 1*)
We are climbing (*BBC Come and Praise 1*)

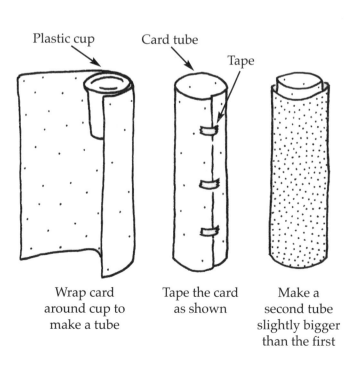

Plastic cup   Card tube   Tape

Wrap card around cup to make a tube

Tape the card as shown

Make a second tube slightly bigger than the first

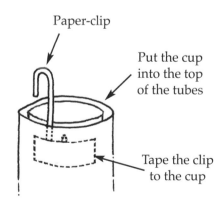

Paper-clip

Put the cup into the top of the tubes

Tape the clip to the cup

Use the paper-clip as a hook to keep the cup in place when you put the tubes down to throw the mug of 'water' at the children

Nicodemus

Preparation

Bring in some breakfast items (e.g. a breakfast bowl with cereal and milk; or toast and marmalade) for the start of the assembly. Alternatively, make a caterpillar from an extendable children's play tunnel, with a large cut-out head stuck to one end. You might like to introduce the assembly with a short excerpt from *The Very Hungry Caterpillar* or 'Naughty Cecil' (a counting song about a caterpillar written and produced by K. Bolam, on a compilation CD and Cassette: see Resources on page 105).

For the Application section you will need a sheet of absorbent kitchen roll or blotting paper, a dark coloured water-soluble pen and a glass or tray of water.

Themes

Spiritual hunger
The need to develop spiritually
Jesus satisfies

Bible references

John 3:1-21; 19:38-42 (a link may also be made with John 7:37-39)

Bible story

Begin with the hungry caterpillar or by eating your breakfast as the children arrive. If you choose the second way in, apologise, but say that you just had to eat because you were *so* hungry.

Explain that this morning you want to talk about hunger. If we are hungry, we try to find something to eat, until we are happy and full. Tell the children that often we think of hunger in terms of food. But we can be hungry in other ways too.

Ask the children to raise their hands if they like computers. Say that we can be hungry to learn more about computers. We may wish to be better at using a computer, hungry to develop our ability, to get better at a particular game or at using the keys or the control console on a game.

Put your hand up if you like PE. We can be hungry to learn more about PE, hungry to develop our skills – to be fitter, to be physically able to achieve more. Show a picture of a well-known athlete or football player and explain how they will have to train in order to get better. Explain to the children that hunger drives us to do things. The athlete trains hard because he or she is hungry to compete with others and to do well.

So there are different kinds of hunger. What would happen if the Hungry Caterpillar or the athlete lost his or her hunger? Explain that they would stop growing or developing.

There is another kind of hunger to think about. Tell the story and ask the children to guess what it is. Use the story in John 3 to tell the children that there was a man – a leader – called Nicodemus. He was what we call a Pharisee. Now most of the Pharisees hated Jesus. They didn't like him. They didn't like the things Jesus said or did.

But Nicodemus could see that there was something special about Jesus. So Nicodemus watched him from a distance. He listened to Jesus carefully as he spoke to crowds of people. He could see that Jesus was very close to God. Nicodemus felt hungry. He was hungry to know more about Jesus. But because he was a Pharisee he wasn't sure that he wanted to be seen with Jesus. What would the other Pharisees say? So, he went to see Jesus at night, when it was dark and quiet. Nicodemus walked in the shadows, until at last he came to the place where Jesus lived.

'Teacher,' he said to Jesus, 'you are very close to God. Tell me more.' Nicodemus felt he was missing something, and he was hungry to know more.

Ask the children what sort of hunger Nicodemus had. (*Take suggestions*)

Nicodemus knew that Jesus could help satisfy his hunger for God. He knew that Jesus could help him get closer to God. Later, in the Bible, we hear more about Nicodemus. And when we see him again, he's not afraid to be seen with Jesus. We can see that Nicodemus has grown. He has a better understanding of Jesus and of God, and he's a stronger person. What would have happened if Nicodemus had ignored that hunger? (*Take suggestions from the children*) Explain that Nicodemus would not have grown spiritually. He would not have grown closer to God in the way that he did.

Application Encourage the children to think about spiritual hunger with a short chromatography experiment. Tear off a strip from the sheet of kitchen roll (the width of the strip will depend on the size of your water receptacle. You should be able to lower the strip into the container without touching the sides). Draw a matchstick figure about 2cm from the bottom edge of the paper (if this proves too difficult with the pen available, simply draw a straight line across the end of the strip, again 2cm from the end).

Explain to the children that God puts a hunger in all of us – a hunger to know him better. Show the children the matchstick figure, and say that it represents us. But if the towel is just left on the table nothing will happen to the figure. Now lower one end (the end with the ink figure) into the water. *Make sure that figure is **above** the water.*

You might like to ask for a volunteer to hold the paper steady as you talk. Explain that the water will soak up into the towel. But what else will it do? It will take the ink along with it: the figure will thus appear to grow upwards (*To allow sufficient time for this to happen, you could sing a song whilst your volunteer holds the strip in the water. The speed will depend on the absorbency of the paper used*).

Tell the children that Jesus is like that water. When he is in our lives he can help satisfy our hunger and helps us to grow up towards God. If necessary, hold the sheet of paper out of the water for all to see.

End by encouraging the children to think about hunger during the day. Ask the children: 'What are you hungry for? Are you hungry for knowledge? Hungry for success? Hungry for fame? Hungry for God? Which hunger will you try to satisfy?'

Closing prayer

Dear God,

Thank you that you put a hunger in all of us to find you. We thank you that Jesus came to satisfy that hunger. Help *us* all to grow . . . that we may know you better and love you more day by day.

Amen.

Suggested songs

Abba Father (*Junior Praise, Kidsource*)
Ask! Ask! Ask! (*Junior Praise*)
Colours of day (*Junior Praise, BBC Come and Praise 1*)
Find the silence through the noise (*Kidsource*)
F-U-N-E-N-R-G? (*Kidsource*)
I want to walk with Jesus Christ (*Junior Praise*)
Lord Jesus Christ (*Junior Praise*)
Seek ye first the kingdom of God (*Junior Praise, Kidsource*)
Water of life (*BBC Come and Praise 1*)
We are climbing (*BBC Come and Praise 1*)
We need to grow (*Kidsource*)

Jairus' daughter

Thoughts This assembly outline could be linked to a particular struggle in the world or local community. It may be used to encourage faith and hope. The outline works particularly well if acted out by one person, who plays the role of Jairus. Simple clothes, such as sandals and a large coat may help. In the script Jairus leaves the room a couple of times to give the feeling of movement and the passage of time. At the places marked *exit* it may also be appropriate to sing a hymn (preferably announced by another adult at the front).

At the end of the story, encourage the children to ask Jairus questions. This may further their understanding of the character and story.

Themes
Jairus' daughter
Healing
God's power to transform
Hope and trust in God

Bible references
Matthew 9:18-26
Luke 8:40-56
(*note:* the Bible does not actually tell us the name of Jairus' daughter)

Preparation Stick newspaper headlines on the wall featuring bad news and good news.

For the Application section you may like to use the rope illusion called *The Professor's Nightmare* (see diagram). You will need a length of rope. Cut the rope into three different lengths: 36cm (short), 62cm (medium) and 90cm (long). Hold the ropes in your left hand like this – S, M and L (with S being closest to your wrist), between your thumb and first finger. Grip the bottom end of the short rope (S) and take it round the M and L ropes. Place the end of the S rope next to the other three ends in your hand (so that you have the ends SSML in your hand).

Now take the bottom end of the medium rope and the longest rope, one at a time, and fold them towards your right. You will now have the six ends of rope in your left hand (SSMLML). Holding the ropes in your left hand, divide them in half. Take the three ends LML with your right hand and pull them slowly apart. Drop the ends in your right hand and the ropes will appear to be of the same size. If you hide the loop with the small rope under your thumb, both sides of your hand may be shown freely.

Bible story   *(Told in role as Jairus)*

(Jairus sits at the front, and appears not to notice the children arrive for the assembly. He is obviously worried about something)

Sorry . . . I don't mean to be rude. I'm Jairus. I'm just worried about my daughter Naomi. She's very ill and she's been in bed for days.

What am I going to do? She's getting worse. The doctors can't help . . . and I've seen the look on their faces before. They don't think . . . they don't think there's any hope. She's only 12 years old.

No hope.

That is . . . could it be? Could it be that Jesus could help? Well, I've heard stories about him. Naomi watched him at a wedding in Cana – we were guests there you see. She watched Jesus have the jars filled with water. I wasn't sure whether to believe her at first – water changed into wine. How she moaned she couldn't taste the wine! But after all these stories maybe she was telling the truth. Maybe it's true what they say about him. Maybe if I can just find him . . . he'll help.

(Exit)

He's there! *(Point across the room as if Jesus were standing there)*

Jesus! Jesus! Naomi, my daughter . . . she's dying. Please, she's all we have in this world. If you just put your hands on her – I believe she'll get well again.

(An imaginary crowd beg for Jesus' attention) No! I asked for help. No, Jesus don't help her now . . . it's my daughter, she's dying and . . . Jesus? Will you come? All these people wanting your attention . . . there's so little time.

(An imaginary person gives Jairus a message. He turns away from Jesus to listen) What? She's died, you say? Naomi's dead . . . my daughter?

Jesus . . . it's too late . . . no one can help now. If only I had come earlier . . .

(Pause to allow time for Jesus to 'speak' to Jairus) I'm listening . . . only believe, you say. Yes . . . I will, Jesus. My home is this way. Oh . . . he's sent the crowds away. Jesus, it's this way . . . *(Exit)*

My home . . . I feel so numb. All these people crying outside. Can I really believe in Jesus?

What? Naomi's sleeping, you say? No Jesus, she can't be, she was very ill, and . . .

Does her hand feel cold, Jesus? There's no life in it.

Little girl, get up? You asked her to get up?

She's breathing . . . yes . . . she's breathing. She's alive! Naomi.

Jesus . . . how did you? How can I ever thank you enough?

Yes. I'll get her something to eat . . .

There's so many people I must tell about Naomi . . . *and* Jesus.

I can't explain it, but I somehow see God in him.

(An adult/teacher now invites the children to ask Jairus questions. Once the questions have finished, the person playing Jairus may like to step out of role.)

Application

Demonstrate the trick *The Professor's Nightmare.* Impossible though it may seem, the ropes changed lengths! They were transformed. Of course this is a simple trick, but it helps us to think about God who really can change things.

Encourage the children to think about Jairus and his daughter. Everything was going well for him . . . everything, that is, until his daughter became ill. His only hope was to go to Jesus and ask for help.

But an enormous crowd surrounded Jesus. Everyone wanted to talk to Jesus. It was so hard to get Jesus on his own. And then a messenger arrived with terrible news: 'Your daughter has died.' It was too late! Perhaps if Jairus had gone for Jesus earlier things would have been different.

But Jesus turned to Jairus and said: 'There is still hope. Take me to your house.'

Jairus could have said: 'Don't be silly. There's nothing either you or anyone else can do. It's too late.' But he didn't. He trusted Jesus and he trusted God.

Emphasise the difference Jesus made to the situation. With him change is possible. Jairus had heard such bad news about his daughter. Yet Jesus could still help.

Explain that the story reminds us that when we hear bad news, Jesus can still help. (You may wish to highlight the news headlines on the wall at this point.) Whether it's bad news in the world or something we're struggling with, we can always ask God to help change the situation and work things out for the good of all.

Closing prayer

End the assembly with the Lord's Prayer. Say the Lord's Prayer slowly, emphasising that we are asking for God's Kingdom to come. You may like to use the following litany:

'Your Kingdom come, your will be done in (*name the place*) as in heaven', e.g. 'Your Kingdom come, your will be done in Liverpool as in heaven.'

'Your Kingdom come, your will be done in Holy Trinity School as in heaven.'

In effect, we are praying for the situation to change (to be delivered from war; for peace to reign etc).

Suggested songs
Go, tell it on the mountain (*Junior Praise, BBC Come and Praise 1*)
I believe in Jesus (*Kidsource*)
I danced in the morning (longer version) (*BBC Come and Praise 1*)
Jairus' daughter (music based on the story by Roger Jones)
Jesus Christ is here (*BBC Come and Praise 1*)
Jesus' hands were kind hands (*Kidsource*)
Jubilate, everybody (*Junior Praise*)
Oh! Oh! Oh! How good is the Lord (*Junior Praise, Kidsource*)
Who took fish and bread? (*Junior Praise*)
You shall go out with joy (*BBC Come and Praise 1*)

Philip and James

Note: The festival of Philip and James falls on 1 May. Philip and James were both apostles, though little is known about them. The James being remembered here is James the son of Alphaeus (otherwise known as James the Less), as opposed to James, the son of Zebedee.

Preparation You will need two coloured table-tennis balls, a length of rope, and a similar length of dark thread. Tie one end of the thread to one end of the rope. Do the same with the other end, so that you form a loop. Use the forefinger of each hand to hold the loop of thread tight behind the rope, forming a double track along which the ball rolls (see diagram). This may require some practice but the effect is well worth it. The children will see you balance a table-tennis ball on the rope, and roll it from one end to the other, like a tightrope walker, without it falling off. (If there is no rope available, the illusion can work, with practice, using a length of dowel, even the edge of a ruler. To attach the thread, simply tie it or tape it.)

For the Application section you will also need a belt and two or three clothes pegs (preferably plastic ones with grooves on them).

Bible story When Jesus started his work, he called 12 people to work with him; 12 people who were to become his friends. We call them disciples. A disciple is a learner or a student.

This morning we're going to be thinking about just two of Jesus' disciples, called . . . Philip and James. (If you do this assembly on or near 1 May, you may wish to refer to the festival of Philip and James in the church's year.)

Explain that we don't know a lot about Philip and James. We don't know what Philip and James looked like. We don't even know what they did for a living – the Bible doesn't tell us. A number of Jesus' disciples were fishermen, so perhaps they were also in the fishing trade. But we can't be sure. What we do know is that when Jesus came along and called them to be his disciples, to be his students, both Philip and

James left their jobs – they left their homes and families, they left everything behind, to follow Jesus.

Application Say how hard that must have been. Ask the children to imagine leaving what they know, their work and family in order to follow Jesus. Where would Jesus lead? What would it involve?

Encourage the children to think about what it must have been like, using the rope and ball illustration. Let one table-tennis ball represent Philip, and the other James (*it is preferable to have two different colours to distinguish them*). Jesus called them both to follow him, and they left all they had to do so.

Place the ball (Philip) on top of the rope and thread. When Jesus came along, their lives were never the same again (*lift the rope, holding it tight, so that the rope and ball are raised together*). Philip and James learnt to trust Jesus with their lives . . . even though at times they didn't know where he was leading them (*allow the ball to roll slowly from one side to the other*). At times Philip and James couldn't understand what Jesus was doing. Jesus took them to new places and showed them new things. They trusted Jesus with their lives, and left everything else behind.

Jesus led his friends over here, and taught them many things (*roll ball back along the rope*). He led his friends over there and taught them many things. The disciples watched Jesus at work. They heard him say many wise things. They were following Jesus and learning from him. But they were just the same as you and I. They had a lot to learn.

Emphasise the point that Jesus didn't call them to follow him on their own. He called them to work together. Sadly, that didn't always happen! Sometimes they quarrelled, and sometimes they wanted the best for themselves. On one occasion, they all got quite cross with each other:

(You might like to ask two children to say alternate lines here)
- *I'm* the most important disciple.
- You're what? Why should *you* be the most important?
- Because Jesus chose *me* first. *I* was the first one he called to follow him.
- No he didn't. Jesus called *me* first. He spoke to me as I was fishing, remember?
- (*looking anxious*) . . . Well . . . *I'm* the most important disciple because he's given *me* the most important job to do. *I* look after the purse with all the money.
- Big deal. *I'm* the oldest . . . and as the oldest *I* should be given the best place.
- No that's for *me*. When *I* get to heaven, *I'm* going to sit next to Jesus.
- Why should *you* be allowed the best seat? What about *me*?

And so they argued. That's not fair . . . this isn't fair. Jesus had to stop them arguing. Sometimes friends do get cross with each other and argue. But Jesus stopped them arguing because when he called his disciples, he didn't want them to squabble with each other. He wanted them to work together. He wanted them to help one another on their journey of discipleship.

Application Ask for two volunteers. See if they can balance a peg right on the end of their finger, so that most of it is hanging in mid-air. Can they do it without the peg falling to the floor?

Produce your belt and ask if that can help. Clip the peg onto the belt so that both sides hang down (the peg needs to be closer to the buckle end of the belt than the end with the holes so that it will balance – see diagram). Now place the peg onto your forefinger. The peg should now sit on your finger (*if it slips off, you can hold it in place by allowing your fingernail to catch in a groove on the peg*).

Explain that the peg is balanced on your finger, and the belt is hanging in mid-air – something that neither of them could have done before. The belt helps the peg to balance.

Jesus calls us to follow him. But emphasise the fact that he calls us to follow him *together*; to travel the road *together* – so that we can support one another; and to do things together that we can't do alone.

Ask the children to go on thinking about that during the day by giving them a question: 'How can they help their friends to follow Jesus?'

Closing prayer *Dear God,*

We pray that you would help us live our lives with you. Help us, like Philip and James, to know the importance of travelling together. Help us to have courage as we face new challenges along the way. May we also encourage and inspire others by our example.

Amen.

Suggested songs A man for all the people (*BBC Come and Praise 1*)
Break out (*BBC Come and Praise 2*)
Brothers and sisters (*Junior Praise*)
Can we love one another (*Kidsource*)
From heaven you came (*Kidsource*)
God loves you (*Kidsource*)
I danced in the morning (*Junior Praise, BBC Come and Praise 1*)
Let us praise God together (*Junior Praise*)
Make me a channel of your peace (*Kidsource, Junior Praise, BBC Come and Praise 2*)
One more step (*Junior Praise, BBC Come and Praise 1*)

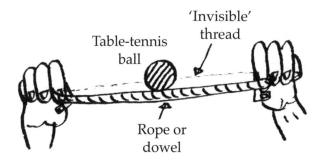

'Invisible' thread

Table-tennis ball

Rope or dowel

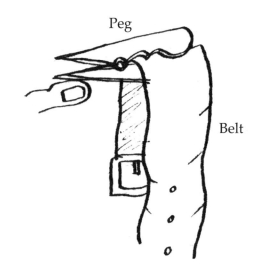

Peg

Belt

The life of Paul

Preparation
You will need two sheets of A4 card. On one card draw or, if you have access to a computer, print a large square (the size does not matter too much – just make sure it is big enough to be seen by all). Inside the square draw or print an arrow, as shown on page 45. Repeat the exercise, making a second square with arrow. Cut out both squares and glue them back to back so that the arrows are visible on both sides and are at right angles to each other. Once the visual aid is finished, try holding the square by the corners that are diagonally opposite each other. Spin the card round. Notice which way the arrows point. Now swap corners. This time the arrows will appear to point in a different direction! The direction of the arrows will depend on which two corners you hold. For ease of use, mark the corners in pencil. This will help you to use the card in the assembly.

For the Application section, you will need to prepare a simple letter. Write the message: 'God loves you. You should be kind and loving too' in bold letters on a plain piece of paper. Without folding the paper, place it inside a new envelope and seal it. You will also need an empty kitchen roll and a good light source (e.g. a window).

Themes
The Christian journey
Sharing God's love
Living for God
Running the race

Bible references
The key verse is Philippians 3:14 (reflections on Paul's life, e.g. Acts 9:1-25; 16:16-40; 19:21-41; 23:12-22; 27:13-44)

Bible story
Many children will be familiar with the *We're Going on a Bear Hunt* story by Michael Rosen and Helen Oxenbury (© 2001 Walker Books, various versions also available from the internet). You might like to use this as a rap, to involve the children. Simply say a line at a time and ask the children to repeat. During each verse, everyone slaps their hands on their knees in a rhythm as if they were marching. You may even like to vary the speed as the story progresses!

Hunting for lions or bears is scary! Explain that a man named Paul went on many scary journeys. He was one of Jesus' followers in the years when the church was just beginning. He didn't go on any lion hunts, but he still faced some frightening situations! He felt that God had given him a special job to do. He felt that he should tell people the good news about God's love. That meant lots of travelling – journeys over land and journeys across the sea.

Paul went to many different countries. His work was often hard and dangerous, and he had to face many problems. Ask the children if they think he carried on his journey (*show arrows pointing the same way*), or did he turn back . . . did he run in the opposite direction when things became difficult? (*Show arrows pointing in opposite directions*)

Let's see what happens as we hear a little bit about Paul's life (*you might like to ask a child in advance to read this*):

> 'My journeys were often hard and dangerous. Some people hated me and the things I said. They stirred up trouble for me – calling me a liar and saying terrible things about me. On one occasion they even dragged me out of a city and threw big stones at me. They left me for dead.
>
> But God loves me and he was with me. Did I give up? No. I simply trusted God even more. I was often cold, hungry and thirsty. At times I even had nowhere to sleep. But I was always so glad I could work for God.'

Application   Paul was thrown into prison several times for what he felt God was calling him to do. (*Show the card with the arrows pointing in different directions*) Did Paul give up? No. Paul still wanted to go God's way. (*Show arrows pointing the same way*) He still wanted to do what God was asking him to do. But how could he when he was in prison? How could he continue to tell people about God?

Well, Paul realised that he could write about God instead. He wrote many letters. What sort of things did he write about? (*Take some suggestions*)

Now ask a volunteer to hold your sealed letter. Tell everyone that there is a secret letter inside. Without opening the envelope, ask if the volunteer can tell you what the letter says?

Ask them to place the kitchen roll against the envelope, and to face a good source of light. They should be able to read: 'God loves you. You should be kind and loving too' – without opening the envelope! Confirm by opening the envelope.

Paul wrote letters telling people how much God loved them. He told them that they should be kind and loving too. It was such a good message he didn't want to keep it a secret. He wanted to tell as many people as possible!

Paul wrote letters to many churches around the Mediterranean. His letters were so good that they were kept, and they even became part of the Bible. His letters helped churches when they faced difficulties . . . encouraging them not to turn back (*use card with arrows pointing in opposite directions*) but to work hard and to press on towards the goal of making the good news of God's love known (*show arrows pointing the same way*).

Closing prayer Father God, we thank you for the life of Paul. Thank you that he was so eager to share the news of your love with other people in different countries. Help us always to remember that you love us too.

Amen.

Suggested songs Give me oil in my lamp (*Junior Praise, Kidsource, BBC Come and Praise 1*)
Go, tell it on the mountain (*Junior Praise, BBC Come and Praise 1*)
One more step (*Junior Praise, BBC Come and Praise 1*)
Seek ye first (*Junior Praise, Kidsource*)
The journey of life (*BBC Come and Praise 1*)
Travel on (*BBC Come and Praise 1*)
We are climbing (*BBC Come and Praise 1*)

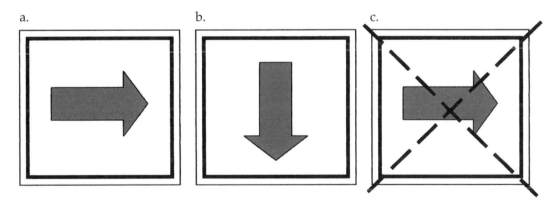

Glue two identical cards (a + b) back-to-back, with the arrows at 90° to each other. When the card is finished, spin by either set of corners as shown in c, and observe the effect.

First steps

Preparation Bring in a wheelbarrow (preferably a clean one!). Place some brown parcel tape across the front of the hall (say three to four metres long) – this is will act as your 'rope' for the assembly. Make sure the tape is not the type that will take the school's proudly varnished floor with it when you remove it. You may also wish to place some chairs at each end, covered with white cloth to simulate rocks, and play a CD with the *Mission Impossible* theme tune.

Themes
| Baptism
| Trust in God
| Faith
| Following God

Bible references
| Daniel 6 (Daniel's faith in God)
| Acts 27 (Paul trusts God, even when shipwrecked)

Bible story As you begin to talk, you might like to stand in the barrow or wheel it around occasionally to add intrigue. Begin by saying that when people come to believe in God – when they say 'Yes, I want to follow God', something special happens. They are what we call 'baptised'. It's a very special time in someone's life, a time when friends and family come together to be with that person and to support them.

A baptism happens in church. When someone is baptised, they're saying: 'I believe and trust in God. I want to live in a way that makes God happy. I believe him and trust him with my life.'

To help the children to think about that, tell the story about a Frenchman called The Great Blondin. Blondin was a tightrope walker. He would walk on nothing more than a thin wire rope strung tightly between two supports. He was so brave, because just one slip and he would fall. He could walk large distances on a tightrope, but he is most famous for walking across the Niagara Falls. People came from far and wide to watch him.

Blondin would carry all sorts of things over the water. Ask the children to imagine that we have the Niagara Falls at the front! Walk along your tightrope and say that the crowd of people watched Blondin walk over, and they watched him return. The crowd clapped and shouted for more.

Then Blondin asked: 'Who believes I can take this wheelbarrow over the waterfall?' One man shouted very loudly: 'Of course you can!'

Blondin took the wheelbarrow over (*demonstrate with the wheelbarrow, taking care to move along the line made by the tape on the floor*). Everyone was very excited.

'Do you believe I can carry this sack of potatoes over the waterfall in the wheelbarrow?' asked Blondin. 'Yes!' the man shouted loudly. Blondin did. Then he asked: 'Who believes I can carry a person over the falls in this barrow?' 'I do!' the man shouted loudly again.

'Then,' said Blondin, 'will you get into my barrow and let me take you across?' There was an embarrassed silence, and the man walked away.

At the same time a little old lady pushed her way through the crowd and got into his wheelbarrow. Blondin pushed her over the falls and back again, to the amazement of the crowd. The lady was Blondin's mother.

Application   Explain that you are going to try, with your barrow, to go across the falls. Ask for a volunteer (it might be advisable to ask someone in advance, and even have a practice so that you don't tip them out by mistake). Play the *Mission Impossible* music as you cross, and ask the children to see if you can do it!

Blondin told the truth. He said he could do it and he did. The man said he trusted Blondin, but proved by his actions that he didn't. Blondin's mother, on the other hand, said she trusted Blondin, and demonstrated it.

Explain that baptism is a little bit like that. It's a way of saying: 'I believe and trust God with my life. I believe that he will keep me safe.'

You might like to talk a little about a baptism service. Ask the children if they have been to a baptism. Explain that you wouldn't normally have a wheelbarrow in church, but that it does involve some water. The person to be baptised will say, in front of friends and relatives, that they believe and trust in God, and in his Son, Jesus Christ. They also make a promise to follow Jesus. Perhaps show some pictures of a font and someone being baptised (you might need to say that people are often baptised as a baby. As they are just a few months old, they can't make those promises for themselves, so parents and friends make them on their behalf, and then encourage the baby, as he or she grows older, to trust in God and to follow Jesus).

Closing prayer   *Dear God,*

In your love, you have called us to know you. Please help us to trust you, and to follow you.

Amen.

Suggested songs

Be bold, be strong (*Kidsource, Junior Praise*)
I walk by faith (*Kidsource*)
I want to walk with Jesus Christ (*Junior Praise*)
Make me a channel of your peace (*Junior Praise, BBC Come and Praise 2*)
One more step (*Junior Praise, Kidsource, BBC Come and Praise 1*)
He who would valiant be (*Junior Praise, BBC Come and Praise 1*)

Breakfast on the beach

Preparation   You will need a table with the following cereals on it (if you can't get them all, a selection of boxes will do):

Apricot Bites, Cheerios, Choco, Clusters, Crunchy, Frosties, Fruitful, Just Right, Monster Cereal, No Problem O's, Perfect Balance, Puffed Wheat, Oatso Simple, Shreddies, Special K, Sporties, Start, Sustain, Vitality and Weetabix.

Keep the items covered with a cloth until you are ready to begin, and lift each item as you get to it in the story.

If you wish to use the closing illustration (see under Application) you will also need a tall, clean glass, a carbonated drink (preferably a new can or bottle), and some plastic tiddlywinks or buttons. The illustration will work with tiddlywinks or buttons of any size, but they need to be clean and free from grease.

> **Themes**
> Post-resurrection appearance
> Jesus is alive
>
> **Bible reference**
> John 21:1-14

Bible story   If you have been looking at the Easter story, you may wish to recap. Explain that at the first Easter, Jesus' friends had seen him die on a cross. They saw him being buried in a cave . . . a tomb. But now Jesus' friends were excited because they knew that he had also risen from the dead. They had seen him full of life and **Vitality**!

'I wonder when we'll see him again,' said one friend.

'Perhaps we won't,' said another. 'Perhaps we have said our **Cheerios** to Jesus for good?'

Some time later, one **Frosties** night, Peter, one of Jesus' friends, decided to go fishing on Lake Galilee. 'Are you coming?' he said to the others. 'What . . . now?'

'Look,' said Peter, 'be **Sporties** . . . it should be a **Fruitful** night. We've got the **Perfect Balance** of weather. It'll be a **Monster** catch . . . we'll catch lots of fish!'

So . . . off they went. The cold grass was **Crunchy** underfoot. They got into a **Cluster** in one boat to keep warm. They went out into the middle of the lake and let out their net . . . but they didn't catch a thing.

'It should **Start** getting light soon,' said Peter, yawning. Then they heard someone call from the beach: 'Have you caught any fish?'

'No . . . we've not had a single (**Apricot**) **Bite**,' they said. 'And we thought the weather was **Just Right**. What's more, we can hardly **Sustain** this as we feel so tired.'

'**No problem O**' said the man on the beach. 'It's **Oatso Simple**. Let down the net – on the other side.'

They pulled the net back in, and did just as the man told them. And they caught so many fish the net was **Choco**-block. In fact the net was almost torn to **Shreddies**. 'It's Jesus!' John whispered to Peter. 'Yes . . . I can see him,' said Peter. 'He always did have that **Special (K)** touch.'

Jesus had lit a small fire on the beach. 'I'll **Start** to cook breakfast,' he said. 'Come and bring some of the fish you have just caught.'

'That's not **Oatso Simple**!' said Peter, as he **Puffed (Wheat)** and panted, trying to drag the net ashore. 'I wish I'd had my **Weetabix** this morning!' he thought. Jesus said to them: 'Come and eat!'

So, they **Cluster**ed around Jesus. 'This is excellent,' thought Peter. And together they had a good breakfast, with plenty to eat.

But none of the friends dared to ask him: 'Who are you?' because they all knew that it was Jesus. This was the third time Jesus appeared to his friends after he came back to life from the tomb.

Application   That's the end of the story about Jesus after Easter – a story about Jesus meeting with his friends after he came back to life.

Let's think about that a little more. I wonder what Jesus and his friends had to drink, when they were together on the beach for a picnic breakfast? The Bible doesn't actually tell us.

Perhaps I can ask you that question. What would you have to drink, if you were having breakfast on a beach somewhere? (*Take suggestions*)

I have a bottle of . . . (*the name of whatever you've got*)

Pour the drink into the glass. Now show the children your plastic tiddly-winks or buttons. One button can represent Jesus. Place the button in the drink. It will sink to the bottom of the glass. As bubbles adhere to the button, it will rise to the surface. Explain that this helps us to remember that Jesus died. But that wasn't the end, because he rose again. He came back to life, and he walked, talked and had meals with his friends. Ask the children to go on thinking about that during the day.

Closing prayer

Dear God,

We thank you that Jesus is alive today. Thank you that you love us, teach us, and hear us when we pray. Help *us* to believe in our heads and know in our hearts that you are with us.

Amen.

Suggested songs

Colours of day (*Junior Praise, BBC Come and Praise 1*)
Come and praise the Lord our King (*Junior Praise, BBC Come and Praise 1*)
God's not dead (*Junior Praise, Kidsource*)
Go, tell it on the mountain (*Junior Praise, BBC Come and Praise 1*)
Jesus isn't dead anymore (*Kidsource*)
Lord of the dance (*Junior Praise, BBC Come and Praise 1*)
When Jesus walked in Galilee (*BBC Come and Praise 1*)

Jesus ascended into heaven

Preparation

On A4 or A3 paper, copy the following road signs from the Highway Code:

30mph speed limit
Road works
Danger ahead
Crossroads
No entry
Picnic site
Traffic lights
School crossing.

You will also need a helium-filled balloon (preferably unadorned) for the Bible story and Application.

Themes

The ascension
The end of Jesus' ministry

Bible references

Acts 1:6-11
Psalm 47:1-9
Philippians 2:1-11
Luke 24:36-53

Bible story

Ask for volunteers to hold up the road signs and see if the children can identify them. Explain the importance of signs. For example, they help us to travel safely. They warn us about things on the road ahead, such as traffic lights and pedestrian crossings. Signs are important. They tell us something in a simple way.

Summarise Jesus' life and ministry using the road signs as a tool. Jesus began his work (point to **roadworks**) when he was about 30 years old (**30mph**). And he called 12 people to be his disciples. He taught them (**school crossing**) about God's Kingdom. He taught them about God's love. But more than that, he showed them God's love. And he gave them many signs as to what God's love is like. But the best sign that God loves us is the cross (**crossroads**). The cross is a sign, a reminder that Jesus, God's Son, died at that first Easter, because God loves us. Jesus died so that we could be forgiven for the wrong things we do in our lives and so that we can be friends with God.

But that wasn't the end (**no entry**). Jesus rose from the dead, and the Bible tells us of a number of occasions when he walked, talked and ate with his disciples. On one occasion he even had a picnic breakfast (**picnic site**) with his friends on a beach.

Then Jesus gave them one last sign. Jesus was with his friends, and he explained to them that the work (**roadworks**) he was sent to do was finished.

'I have done all that God wanted me to do,' said Jesus.

'Go and tell everyone about me. Tell them everything that I have told you: how God wants to rescue them (**danger ahead**) and make them safe.'

When Jesus spoke to them they were just outside Jerusalem on the mountain of Olives. 'Don't leave Jerusalem just yet,' said Jesus. 'Wait until God sends you another Helper. Then go (**traffic lights**), and tell the whole world about me. Make me lots more friends.'

The disciples looked at each other. 'But Jesus, when will you be our king?' asked one.

'When will you come back?' asked another.

Jesus smiled and said: 'God will decide.'

Jesus was still speaking when he started to rise into the sky. The disciples watched as he was taken up into the heavens, and then the clouds hid him from their sight.

(Release balloon out of a window)

Close the story by saying that the disciples were looking up at the sky when two men, dressed in white, suddenly stood beside them. They said: 'Why are you gazing into the sky? Jesus has gone home to be with God, his Father. But one day he will come back.'

Application Explain that we remember Jesus' ascension (rising up) on Ascension Day, 40 days after Easter. Point out that Jesus ascending (going up) into heaven was a sign that his work was finished. Jesus had done all that God had sent him to do. Jesus could have been taken into heaven at night while everyone was asleep. But it was important for people to see him ascend, as it was a sign that his work was done.

Ask the children if they can all see the balloon. For some children, the balloon may now be out of sight. But reassure them that the balloon is still there!

Ask the children when they think the balloon will come back down to earth? (*Take suggestions*)

The answer is that no one knows! Encourage the children to think about the balloon during the day. It can remind them that Jesus is in heaven . . . and that Jesus, one day, will come back.

'When will you come back?' asked one of Jesus' disciples.

'God will decide,' said Jesus.

No one knows when Jesus will return.

What do we do in the meantime? Jesus left signs in the Bible for us to follow. Jesus gave us signs as to how he wants us to live. He wants us to love God and to love one another. He wants us to tell other people about God. That's the work that he wants us to do, as we wait for Jesus' return.

Closing prayer

Lord Jesus,

We thank you that you ascended as king of heaven and earth. Thank you that you are in control of all things. Help us to trust you and to tell others about you.

Amen.

Suggested songs

Colours of day (*Junior Praise, BBC Come and Praise 1*)
Come and join in the song (*Kidsource*)
Come and praise the Lord our King (*Junior Praise, BBC Come and Praise 1*)
I want to walk with Jesus Christ (*Junior Praise*)
Jesus isn't dead anymore (*Kidsource*)
Lord, I lift your name (*Kidsource*)
Now thank we all our God (*Junior Praise, BBC Come and Praise 1*)
Our eyes have seen the glory (*Junior Praise*)
Who took fish and bread (*Junior Praise*)

When the Spirit came

Preparation   You will need a coloured piece of card, two identical balloons and two drink cans (one empty, the other full).

Bible story   Show the children two balloons and ask if they are the same.

(*Inflate one*) Are they still the same? (*Take suggestions*)

They're still the same colour. They're still made of the same material. They're still both balloons. So what has changed? One is now full of air or wind.

(*Let it deflate, making a strange sound*)

There's a story in the Bible about a strange wind. Invite the children to make the noise of wind every time you hold up the piece of coloured card.

Jesus' friends were all together in a room – when all of a sudden (*hold up coloured card*) (*Whooooo!*) A big wind came (*Whooooo!*) It blew right round the room (*Whooooo!*) And it filled the whole house where they were sitting.

'This is a strange wind,' (*Whooooo!*) they thought. Then they saw what looked like little flames that blew round (*Whooooo!*) The fire touched each person, but no one was hurt.

Jesus' friends started to talk, all at once. They didn't know what they were saying, but they were all speaking different languages!

God's special helper, the Holy Spirit, had come! (*Whooooo!*) Now they would be able to go and tell the whole world about Jesus.

When this happened there was a great holiday called Pentecost, and many people came to Jerusalem from other countries to celebrate. When they heard the noise (*Whooooo!*) a large crowd gathered:

'What's that noise?' (*Whooooo!*) 'What's going on?'

'I can hear someone speaking . . .' said one of them, '. . . about the great things that God has done. But . . . it's in my own language!'

'I can hear it, too!' said another. 'But what does it mean?'

Then Peter, one of Jesus' friends, stood up and spoke to the crowd.

He said: 'This is what God promised us.' Then he told them about Jesus, about the miracles that God performed through him, and how God sent him to show us how we could know more about God.

'But you,' said Peter, 'let him die on a cross.'

When the crowd heard this they were worried and asked: 'What should we do? How can we put things right?'

'Each one of you should tell God that you are sorry,' said Peter, 'and God will forgive you. You can also be Jesus' friends.'

That day about 3000 people became Jesus' friends.

Application   When the Holy Spirit came what did he sound like? (*coloured card*) (*Whooooo!*) He sounded something like a rushing wind. Wind can be very powerful. The noise of the wind suggests power, a force beyond our control. What Jesus' friends received was nothing less than God himself. God was blowing into their lives. It is the same Holy Spirit that comes to blow in our lives. And when that happens, when God blows in our lives, we change (*inflate the other balloon*).

Ask for two volunteers . . .

Encourage the children to think about the change that the Holy Spirit makes by using the two drink cans. Give one to each child. Then ask them to try and crush the cans in one hand. The full, unopened one will not squash.

Explain that the empty can, with nothing in it, is easily crushed. It can't take much pressure before it caves in. It can't stand up to very much. You squeeze, and it struggles to keep its shape.

The full can is like one of the disciples, or one of us, filled with the Spirit. You squeeze and nothing happens. Because what's inside helps to give it strength. When the Holy Spirit is in our lives, he helps to give us strength to follow Jesus. We no longer have to struggle by ourselves, for God can blow his Spirit into us to help us.

Encourage the children to think about God's Spirit during the day.

Closing prayer   Ask the children to make the noise of a gentle wind as you pray:

Come Holy Spirit,

Come and fill us with your love. Come and fill us with your power, so that we may live in a way that pleases you.

Amen.

Suggested All over the world (*Junior Praise*)
songs Colours of day (*Junior Praise, BBC Come and Praise 1*)
Hang on (*Kidsource*)
Jesus, send me the helper (*Kidsource*)
Spirit of God (*BBC Come and Praise 1*)
Spirit of peace (*BBC Come and Praise 2*)
Jesus in the garden (*BBC Come and Praise 2*)
We praise God (*Kidsource*)

This assembly is based on an original idea by Martin Hewitt and is used with permission.

A sticky ending?

Preparation

You will need a table with the following chocolate bars. Keep the items covered with a cloth until you are ready to begin, and lift each item as you get to it in the story . . .

Yorkie, Quality Street, Galaxy, Snickers, Flyte, Whole Nut, Bounty, Crunch, Picnic, Topic, Rolo, Ripple, Smarties, Celebration, Wispa, Flake, Dime, Double Decker.

If you wish to use the closing illustration (see under Application) you will also need two paper bags of the same size and colour. Place some confetti into bag 1. Carefully cut the top off bag 2 and make some small holes in the bottom. Put some glue around the top of the second bag and place it inside the larger one. This double-skinned bag will be used at the end of the story to help the children to think about change.

Themes

Prodigal son
A new start
Forgiveness

Bible reference

Luke 15:11-24

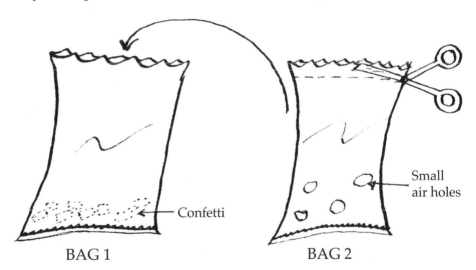

Confetti

Small air holes

BAG 1   BAG 2

Bible story

A long, long time ago, there was a **Yorkie** man who had two sons, James and Ebenezer. The family were all **Yorkie**s, and they lived on **Quality Street**. Ebenezer, the youngest son, decided that one day he would like to be rich. That was the only thing that mattered to him in the whole **Galaxy**.

And so, one day, Ebenezer asked his dad for his share of the money. 'Dad,' he said, 'I want my share of your **Bounty** and I want it now!'

His dad could feel his lips **Ripple**, as he tried to hold back the tears. But he gave him the money. It wasn't long before Ebenezer had packed his bags and left home.

In fact, he left the country. He got a **Double Decker** bus, then a **Flyte**, and went abroad, as far away as he could go.

Then he started to spend his money . . . on parties and trips to other exciting places. He bought several sports cars and made plenty of friends . . . or so he thought. But Ebenezer never really had any friends . . . 'He's a **Whole Nut** case,' they would say. And they would **Snicker** behind his back.

Poor Ebenezer – he wasn't a **Smartie**. The day soon came when his money ran out. He'd spent his last **Dime**. He turned to his friends for help. 'I've given my last **Rolo**' he said: 'I've nothing left' . . . but they didn't want to know him any more.

It was **Crunch** time. Ebenezer decided to get a job . . . the only one he could find was feeding pigs. The job was no **Picnic** . . . it was hard work and very dirty. He was so hungry and tired he nearly **Flake**d out.

There was now only one **Topic** on Ebenezer's mind. What was he going to do?

'This is silly' he **Wispa**red to himself. 'Why don't I go home? No one is hungry there. They all have lots of good things to eat on **Quality Street**. I'll tell Dad I'm sorry I wasted his **Bounty**. I don't deserve to be one of the family. But perhaps he'll let me work for him.'

So he set off for home.

All this time his father had waited and watched for his son to come home. Now here he was coming down the road!

His dad ran out to meet him.

'I'm so sorry, Dad,' Ebenezer said.

But his dad hugged him . . . 'Fetch the boy new clothes,' he shouted. 'We're going to have a party . . . a **Celebration**! My boy has come home and I'm so happy. I thought I'd lost him, but now he is found.'

Application   Explain that this is a story similar to one Jesus told in the Bible. Jesus wanted people to know that God loves them and cares for them.

In the story Ebenezer changed. Saying sorry isn't always easy . . . particularly when you've been silly. But when Ebenezer saw the mess he was in, he said sorry and his dad forgave him. He had a fresh start. He changed his ways.

Let's think about this a little more. I have a piece of plain paper here. What was Ebenezer sorry for? (*Take ideas from the children*):

- Hurting his dad
- Wasting money
- Thinking of himself.

I have some plain paper here. I'll write a few words on it (*write the words Hurt, Waste, Selfish*). Let's scrunch it up and put the sheet into our paper bag.

Ebenezer said sorry to his dad. And his dad forgave him. He changed his ways and had a fresh start. Let's blow up the bag . . . **bang**!

Only the outer bag bursts.

The sheet of paper will appear to have changed – into lots of colourful pieces. When we say sorry life is often better and brighter. We can be happier.

Go on thinking about that during the day. Ask yourself this question – is there anything that I need to say sorry for? It's not always easy to say sorry, but there is bound to be someone we should say sorry to.

Closing prayer

Dear God,

Help *us* to be ready to say sorry, and to admit the mistakes we make. Help us to remember that if we say sorry, we can be forgiven and live more happily together.

Amen.

Suggested songs

God forgave my sin (*Junior Praise*)
It's a new day (*BBC Come and Praise 2*)
Make me a channel (*Kidsource, Junior Praise, BBC Come and Praise 2*)
O Lord, all the world belongs to you (*BBC Come and Praise 1*)
Oh, once there was a father (*Kidsource*)
Spirit of God (*BBC Come and Praise 1*)

Start with what you've got

Preparation   For telling the Bible story you may like to use a large paper wallet with some toy money inside.

For the opening illustration you will need two cardboard boxes: 750g or 1kg cereal boxes are ideal (e.g. about 30cm high, 20cm wide and 10cm deep). Boxes come in all shapes and sizes, but it is important that you find two that nest together reasonably well. With a sharp knife, remove the top flaps of the inner box and make a window as shown in diagram (a). Paint the inside of the box matt black (or line with black paper). Cover the outside of the box with a light-coloured paper. You will also need to make a card partition to go inside the box (with a matt-black finish). This will fit diagonally across the inside of the box, 2cm short of the top. Diagram (c) shows how the partition should look from above. This leaves a secret space at the rear of the box in which to hide small items.

The outer box (b) will need to have both the top and bottom flaps removed. The interior of this box should also be matt black, with a brightly coloured exterior.

> ## Themes
> Feeding of the 5000
>
> Living up to our full potential
>
> Gifts and talents
>
> ## Bible references
> Matthew 14:13-21; 25:14-30
>
> Luke 9:10-17
>
> Mark 6:30-44
>
> John 6:1-14

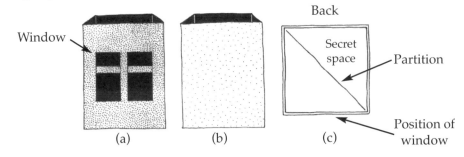

To set the illusion, nest the boxes together with the inner box containing various items (e.g. small scarves, handkerchiefs or flat items), and place on a low table. To create the illusion that the boxes are empty, first pull up the outer box and display the open top-end to the children so that they can see the black interior. Before replacing, put your hand in through the window in the other box to prove that it too is empty. Replace so that the two boxes are nested together again. Now pull out the things that you have hidden in the back!

(Note: for the illusion to work well the children should not be aware that there is a partition inside the box. You may therefore like to keep the box covered with a cloth as the children enter, to stop them peeping in.)

Explain that this is a simple trick. But what a surprise! Jesus was often full of surprises. In the story today the children are going to hear about a miracle that Jesus performed where he produced something amazing!

Bible story   It was getting late. A big crowd of people had listened to Jesus all day. Now everyone was tired and hungry. They were out in the hills, miles from anywhere.

One of Jesus' special friends, called Philip, said to Jesus: 'Jesus, there's nothing here for them to eat. Send them away . . . tell them to go to the farms and villages to buy something there.'

But Jesus said something surprising. Jesus said to Philip: 'You give them something to eat.'

'I . . . I can't do that,' said Philip. 'You want me to buy food for all these people? But there are more than 5000 people here! It would cost far too much.' (*open wallet*) 'Look,' said Philip, 'that's all the money I've got (*hold up toy £20 note*).'

'Ask if they've got any bread,' said Jesus.

So Jesus' friends went round the crowd asking them: 'Have *you* got any bread?'

'Have *you* got any bread?'

But they all shook their heads – all except for one small boy. He had five bread rolls and two small fish to eat.

Philip brought the little boy to Jesus. Without a word the little boy held out his five bread rolls and two small fish for Jesus to take. But the disciples laughed: 'That's not going to go far amongst all these people, is it?'

But Jesus smiled at the boy. The boy had done the right thing.

Jesus always said thank you to God for his food. Even though Jesus only had the little boy's dinner . . . he still thanked God for it.

After that, Jesus shared it with *all* the people. First the bread and then the fish. The little boy couldn't believe his eyes.

Everyone in the crowd had something to eat . . . and not just a crumb, but plenty of dinner.

And there was not just enough . . . but lots left over. At the end of the meal, Jesus' friends went round and picked up 12 baskets full of left-overs!

Application

That's the end of my story: a story about Jesus feeding 5000 people with just a little boy's picnic. To help you remember that story, look at the cross. This is sometimes called the cross of St Philip, because if you look carefully you'll see two circles at the bottom. The circles represent the bread and the fish, and remind us of how Jesus fed a large crowd.

Now Philip wasn't stupid, but Jesus did something with the fish and the bread that surprised him. If we're honest, at times we feel like Philip. Sometimes we can think: 'I can't do that', and at times we don't feel like trying.

But Jesus wants us to think differently. Jesus started with what he'd got. He didn't have much, but he said thank you to God for it. Then Jesus made something of it. He put it to good use, and did amazing things with it.

The story should encourage us to try and make something of what we have. It should encourage us to develop our gifts and abilities – to put them to good use. With God's help our gifts can grow into something wonderful.

End by asking the children who they will be like. Will they be like Philip, who says: 'It can't be done. I can't do it.' Or will they be like Jesus who gave thanks for what was there, and used it.

Closing prayer

Dear God,

Thank you that you have given each one of us different gifts and talents. Give us the determination and strength to try to develop the talents you have entrusted to us. And help us, so that whatever we do or become, we may do it with all our strength and to your glory.

Amen.

Suggested songs

A boy gave to Jesus (*Junior Praise*)
Bread for the world (*BBC Come and Praise 2*)
It's a new day (*BBC Come and Praise 2*)
Spirit of peace (*BBC Come and Praise 2*)
5000+ hungry folk (*Kidsource*)

An attitude problem?

Preparation   On A4 pieces of paper, print the following:

- ☐ kind
- ☐ patient
- ☐ helpful
- ☐ attitude
- ☐ put God first
- ☐ beatitude
- ☐ happiness

Themes
Sermon on the Mount
Beatitudes
Zacchaeus' lifestyle

Bible references
Matthew chapters 4-6; Luke 19:1-10

You will need to enlarge the picture of Zacchaeus onto an A3 sheet of paper. You may also wish to use a ladder in the story of Zacchaeus (if available). The puppet script below may also be used as a way of introducing the theme.

Place some litter on the floor so that the front looks untidy. As a way in, start with your puppet (if you haven't used the puppet before, introduce it to the children by giving it a name. I have used the name Bones in the script below).

Bible story   *You:*   What's been going on, Bones? Just look at all this mess. I asked you to clear it up before the assembly started. Do you know what you are? You are a lazy Bones . . . and that's not meant to be funny.

(*Speaking to the children*) I'm not very happy, because Bones pinched my cereal at breakfast-time this morning.

Bones: I wanted some.

You: That's not the point. You deliberately took it without asking! It's no wonder people don't like you . . . and, come to think of it, I don't like you very much when you behave like this. When you're at school you never want to share the pencil crayons, rubber or ruler with anyone. If the teacher asks you to sit on the carpet, you push your way to the front. And when you get home, you rush to the biscuit tin and pinch all the chocolate biscuits before your sister gets in.

Do you remember you asked me why – on your birthday last week – why no one came to your party? It's because you're so mean and horrible. If you're greedy and unkind, if you're nasty and cheat . . . you won't be happy.

Put Bones down on a chair and explain that *Bones'* behaviour has reminded you of a story about someone called Zacchaeus. Show the children the A3 picture of Zacchaeus, making sure that he looks sad.

Go on to explain how Zacchaeus collected money for the Romans. He was a taxman. He was also a cheat and always made people pay far more than they should. Zacchaeus was fat and rather small. Although he grew richer and richer, he was very unhappy, for Zacchaeus had no friends.

One day Jesus came and people crowded round to see what Jesus had to say. But no one told Zacchaeus what was going on. He thought: 'Oh no! Where is everyone going?'

He rushed outside, but no one would tell him very much. But Zacchaeus didn't stay at home. He followed the crowds. When he reached where they were going, he couldn't see Jesus – his legs were too short to see over the top. He tried pushing his way through, but people wouldn't let him pass. He tried jumping up and down (*jump up and down*) but that didn't help much. Then he had an idea. He stretched up – up to the lowest branch of a tree, and he began to climb (*climb ladder*).

People laughed at him. But to his surprise, when Jesus saw him, he didn't laugh. He looked straight up at Zacchaeus and said: 'Zacchaeus, come down from that tree. I want to come to your house today.' '*My* house?' He couldn't believe his ears. '*My* house!'

He felt so excited as he walked along the street with Jesus, and together they went into his house. As they talked, Zacchaeus felt sorry for the way he'd behaved.

Outside, the people grumbled. 'Why has Jesus gone into *his* house? He's just a nasty little cheat,' they said.

But Zacchaeus didn't want to cheat any more. Jesus was his friend now.

Zacchaeus came out of his house saying: 'I'm going to give half my money away. And I'll pay back everyone I've cheated – four times as much as I took.'

That day Zacchaeus' attitude changed (*point to the word 'attitude'*). His way of thinking changed. The way he treated others changed. But that wasn't the only thing that changed (*now turn Zacchaeus' face up-side-down, to reveal a smile*). Zacchaeus' face changed from being sad to happy. Jesus was his friend. Other people in the town became his friend, too.

Application Finish talking about Zacchaeus. Go on to tell the children that happiness does not simply come from being rich. In order to be happy we need to think of others – to be kind and patient (*point to the words at the front*). Happiness does not come from pushing and grabbing things for yourself.

'The happy person,' Jesus says, 'puts God first and stays true to him.' You might like to add that Jesus talked about having the right sort of attitudes in Matthew chapters 4 and 5. His talk has come to be known as 'the Beatitudes'. Beatitudes simply means 'the attitudes to be at' (i.e. the attitudes we should have).

Closing prayer Tell the children that you are going to pray together by reading out together verses one and two from the song 'Make me a channel of your peace'.

Suggested songs Abba Father (*Junior Praise*)
Light up the fire (*Junior Praise, BBC Come and Praise 1*)
Make me a channel (*Kidsource, Junior Praise, BBC Come and Praise 2*)
Nobody liked Zacchaeus (*Kidsource*)
O Lord, all the world belongs to you (*BBC Come and Praise 1*)
One more step (*Junior Praise, BBC Come and Praise 1*)
Peace, perfect peace (*BBC Come and Praise 1*)
Spirit of God (*BBC Come and Praise 1*)

Parable of the supermarket

Preparation   This assembly works best if acted out. If available, use a toy trolley or similar, and some cans of food on a low table, to set the scene. Before the assembly you might also like to print an imaginary shop name on an A3 sheet of paper, and the words *Biff-bash* on a second sheet for the fight scene.

Themes
Parable of the tenants in the vineyard
Rejecting God's message
God's love
Easter

Bible references
Matthew 21:33-46
Mark 12:1-12
Luke 20:9-18

Bible story   There was once a man who bought a supermarket. Let's call it ACME. (*Point to the child playing the part, so that the children know who the boss is*) There was once a man who bought a supermarket. He let it out to various staff. And then, one day, the owner said to his staff: 'I'm going away . . . probably for some time. Look after things while I'm gone.'

He caught the train, and went on a journey . . . (*get the children to slap their legs to make the noise of a train*). A very long journey south, through the Channel Tunnel, to a faraway land.

Months passed. Our supermarket staff were all working very hard, keeping the supermarket shelves stacked and looking tidy, making sure that there were prices on every item. Lots of people came from the local town to use the store in order to buy food.

Oh look, I think we've got a customer now . . . (*Child walks on and buys some items of food*)

The supermarket did very well.

As time went on, the owner decided to send a friend, someone he trusted, to go back to England to collect the profits. The friend came on the train (*slap legs for train*) . . . through the Channel Tunnel . . . to the north.

But the staff beat the friend and sent him back without a thing (*as the children go to 'fight', screen them with your large Biff-bash sign, and have them make some sound effects such as 'Ouch', 'ow' and 'groan'*).

So the owner sent another friend, someone he trusted very much. He got on the train (*slap legs for train*) . . . through the Channel Tunnel . . . to the north.

But the staff beat this friend as well and sent him back without a thing (*hold up Biff-bash sign again*).

So the owner sent a third friend. He got on the train . . . a fast train (*slap legs faster*) through the tunnel. But the staff beat this friend as well (*Biff-bash sign*). They hurt him and sent him back without a thing.

Then the owner of the supermarket said to himself: 'What shall I do? (*have the owner walk up and down, as if thinking*). I know! I'll send my son, my only son – surely they will treat him well!'

Sure enough, the owner's son got on the train (*slap legs*) . . . but when he came to the supermarket, the staff saw him coming and they said: 'This is the owner's son. Let's kill him and then the store will be ours.' So they threw him out of the back of the store and they killed him.

What will the owner do now? I'll tell you. The owner will come and sack all the staff, and he'll hire new staff in his store, so that it'll be under new management.

Ask the children to think about what the story means. Jesus told a similar story in his day. He told the story just before Easter. Easter is a very important time – ask if anyone knows what happened at Easter.

(Take suggestions from the children)

Jesus was actually telling people in his own day what the situation was. Jesus was saying that God, the shop-owner in the story, had sent lots of messengers to his people, showing them how they could be obedient to God, and telling them how he wanted them to live. God sent messenger after messenger to his people, but each time they were ignored. Worse, they were often beaten up. So, God thought: 'Right, I'll send my own son.'

Jesus said: 'I am that son, and even though I have come to show you how to be obedient to God, you'll have me killed too.'

Jesus knew he was going to be killed at that first Easter. And he was warning them what was going to happen. Jesus was really warning the people, saying: 'Listen to me, before it's too late. Otherwise God will be very angry with you.'

If time permits, tell the version of the story that Jesus told. End by saying that Jesus warned the people to listen to him, before it was too late. How will we respond to Jesus? Will we try to follow his example, as he wants us to?

Closing prayer Lord God, thank you for sending Jesus into the world. Thank you that he came to show us how to be obedient to him. Help us to listen to him, and to live in a way that pleases him.

Amen.

Suggested songs Come and praise the Lord our King (*Junior Praise, BBC Come and Praise 1*)
Down in the jungle (*Kidsource*)
Go, tell it on the mountain (*Junior Praise, BBC Come and Praise 1*)
Lord of the dance (*Junior Praise, BBC Come and Praise 1*)
Think of a world (*Junior Praise*)
When Jesus walked in Galilee (*BBC Come and Praise 1*)

Our Father in heaven

Preparation
Find the names of some roads in the area, ideally those which can be easily recognised, but that can be used to tell the story of Daniel and the lions' den. It might be easiest to use a local street map. Write or print the road names on strips of card and stick them to the wall. I have included the names of roads in my locality, as an example:

Themes
To whom we pray
Father God

Bible reference
Daniel 6:1-28

Achilles, Andover, Armour, Back, Bath, Bluecoat, Bold, Cann, Cardigan, Carpenter, Centurion, Cromwell, Cross, Daniel, East, Egypt, Florida, Friends, Grey, Golbourne, Gregory, Greenfields, Kingsway, Kings, Livingstone, Lord, Lowe, Lyons, Mallard, Matlock, Payne, Peace, Peacocks, Prospect, Quay, Reddish, Refuge, Rock, Roughley, Rush, Sage, Scholars, Small, Topping, Treetops, Valiant, Waring, Well, Westbrook, Wolfe, Whiteleggs, Wright.

For the application section you will also need a strip of paper with the words 'Our Father in heaven' across the middle, and two large paperclips.

Bible story
Ask the children to tell you what these names have in common? Highlight some of the road names you have printed off.

Tell the children that this morning you want them to think about where they live. What is the name of their road? How many houses does it have? What number do they live at?

Think about where you live . . . think about where God lives. What's God's address?

Now use the road names, inserting your own where there are *italics* in the story . . .

A long time ago and far, far away lived a man whose name was . . . (take suggestions for a name: *Cromwell? Livingstone? Gregory?*) *Daniel! Daniel's* story is in the Bible. *Daniel* was living far away from his home in Jerusalem. He had been treated *Roughley* as a prisoner. And he was taken away from his home to live in . . . (*take suggestions from the children . . . Matlock? Egypt? California? Florida? Golborne?*) . . . taken to live in the *East!*, to a place called Babylon. But *Daniel* trusted the *Lord* God and did as God said.

Every day he prayed to God, and God made *Daniel* (*take suggestions from the children until they get the right answer* . . . a *Cardigan*? a *Carpenter*? a *Centurion*?) He made Daniel a *Sage* . . . that means wise. In fact *Daniel* became the wisest of all the *Scholars* in Babylon.

One day, the king chose *Daniel* for a very important job. He was the *King's* favourite. But Daniel's *Prospect* didn't look good. For the other wise men were not *Daniel's Friends*. They were *Cross* and became *Reddish* with jealousy.

But *Daniel* was very *Valiant* – they couldn't scare him. And he always did what was *Wright* – so they couldn't tell tales to the king.

'*Cann* we get rid of him?' they thought. Then one of them had a clever idea.

'*Daniel* wants to please God even more than he wants to please the king. It's his *Achilles* heel.

So this is what we'll do . . .'

Whisper, whisper, whisper.

The wise men of Babylon went to the king.

'O king, live for ever,' they said, bowing *Lowe*. 'We want you to make a new law. Tell everyone they must pray to you only – or be thrown to the (*take suggestions* . . . *Wolfe*? *Mallard* ducks? *Peacocks*? *Lyons*!'

The king did not know it was all a trick to get rid of *Daniel*. So he made the new law – a law that could not be changed.

Daniel soon knew about the king's new law – everyone did. But he wanted to follow God's way even more than he wanted to follow the *Kingsway*. So he prayed to the *Lord* God, as he always did.

The wise men of Babylon saw him, through the *Treetops*, kneeling at his *Small* window. Their plan had worked. Chuckling with glee, they hurried to tell the king.

'O king, live forever,' they said, bowing *Lowe* and pretending to feel sad. 'We bring bad news. *Daniel* has disobeyed your new law. We saw him ourselves, praying to God at his *Small* window. The law is clear. *Daniel* must be thrown to the *Lyons*.'

The king was most upset. But the law could not be changed. He could not save *Daniel*.

The king had to *Andover Daniel* to the *Lyons*. The *Lyons* were hungry and they roared for their supper.

'I do hope God can save you,' the king said to *Daniel*, as they pushed him in with the *Lyons*, and they locked the door with the *Quay*. *Daniel* was *Bold*, because he was *Waring* no *Armour*, just his *Bluecoat*.

The king tried to relax. He had a long *Bath*, and tried to sleep. But all night long he lay awake thinking about *Daniel* – and the *Payne* of being eaten by hungry *Lyons*.

As soon as it was light, the king was in a *Rush*. He looked quite *Grey* with worry. He hurried *Back* to see if *Daniel* was all right. He couldn't hear any noise – just *Peace* and quiet.

'*Daniel, Daniel*!' the king called out. 'Has God been able to save you from the *Lyons*?' He felt sure those hungry *Lyons* had eaten *Daniel* for their supper.

But *Daniel's* voice came back, loud and clear.

'O king, live for ever – I am *Well*! God has been my *Rock* and my *Refuge*.

He has kept me safe all night . . . the *Lyons* haven't opened their mouths once!'

The king shouted out: 'That's *Topping!*'

'Let him out at once!' he ordered. *Daniel* came out. God had saved him from the *Lyons*.

Application Explain that we often say the Lord's Prayer. But what do the words actually mean?

The first line says: 'Our Father in heaven.'

Father is another name for God. By saying 'Our Father in heaven', we're reminding ourselves about whom we are praying to. We're praying to God, who is in heaven . . . that's God's address!

Explain to the children that we're not praying to another person. We're not praying to a king or a queen, as they were in the story. But like Daniel, we pray to God who is in heaven. So the first line of the prayer helps us to focus our minds and to think about whom we're talking to.

Encourage the children to think about this some more.

Using an A4 sheet of paper, print 'Our Father in heaven' in a large font across the middle (in landscape). Trim the paper top and bottom, to make a long strip. In front of the children, bend a third of the paper backwards and put on a large paper-clip. Tell the children that this paper-clip represents 'Our Father God'. Next, bend the remaining third of the paper forwards and put on a second large paper-clip.

Make sure that this second paper-clip only goes on the front two folds (see diagram below). This second paper-clip represents 'us in prayer'. Now pull the two ends of the paper strip. The clips will slide towards each other and link up, before shooting off the paper.

Remind the children what's printed on the paper: 'Our Father in heaven'.

Saying 'Our Father in heaven' helps us to draw near to God in prayer.

Encourage the children to think about those things during the day.

Closing prayer

Dear God,

You are our heavenly Father and we are your children. You love us and teach us how to be like you. You never leave us or get tired of looking after us. Thank you that you always hear us when we pray to you. Help us to love you more for Jesus' sake.

Amen.

The Lord's Prayer

Suggested songs

Dear Lord, my Father who's in heaven (The Lord's Prayer) (*Kidsource*)
Father, hear the prayer we offer (*BBC Come and Praise 1, Junior Praise*)
Have you heard (*Kidsource*)
Lord of all hopefulness (*BBC Come and Praise 1, Junior Praise*)
Safe in the Father's hands (*Kidsource*)
The Lord's Prayer (*Junior Praise, BBC Come and Praise 1*. Also to various settings, e.g. Loaves and fishes)
There once was a man called Daniel (*Kidsource*)

Your kingdom come

Legend After Jesus had finished his work on earth he went up into heaven and was greeted by the Archangel Gabriel. Gabriel was rather worried about the future, so he asked Jesus a question. 'Lord,' he asked, 'What plans have you made for carrying on your work below?' Jesus answered: 'I have chosen 12 men.' Gabriel was even more worried. '*Just* 12 men to continue your work,' Gabriel gasped. 'But what if they should fail? What then?'

Jesus answered simply: 'I have made no other plans.'

Themes
Building the kingdom
God works through us
God's hands

Bible references
Acts 3:1-16 and Acts 4:5-10 (where God uses Peter to heal others)
or Exodus 3:1-12 (God calls Moses to be his representative)
or use the legend which starts this chapter

Preparation If available, place some Bob the Builder merchandise on a table at the front. You might like to display his catchphrase or ask the children to call it out together after dramatically counting: '1 . . . 2 . . . 3 . . .'

For the Bible story, place the following items in a large bag: *clock, basket, money (you could use paper money from a game, for example), empty wallet, tambourine.*

For the application section you will need to make a simple jigsaw puzzle. Make or enlarge a picture of Jesus on to an A3 sheet of paper (a line drawing will do). Make sure your Jesus has no hands. Cut the picture into half a dozen pieces or so, and stick them around the room before the children enter.

Bible story Begin by asking the children to call out Bob the Builder's catchphrase.

Bob the Builder has lots of helpers. Who are they? (*Take suggestions from the children*) Wendy, Scoop, Lofty, Muck, Dizzy, etc. Ask the children what happens when these characters work together. You should have the responses that things get done, are fixed and things get built. (*All together! What's his catchphrase . . .?*)

Explain that you are going to look at the line of the Lord's Prayer that says: 'Your kingdom come . . . on earth as in heaven.'

Challenge the children by asking what it means. Say that in the prayer we are asking for God's kingdom to come. We're praying: 'Let it come . . . let it be built.' We're asking God to build his kingdom here on earth, to change this world and change us. We want him to come and build his kingdom through us. (*All together! What's that catchphrase . . .?*)

Encourage the children to think about God the Builder. Mention that working together, we can get the job done.

That's true of God the Builder. He wants us to work together with him, to build his kingdom – to get the job done. The kingdom is a good place to be.

Tell the children that God wants to work together with us. There's a story in the Bible about two of Jesus' friends. Jesus had asked his friends to carry on his work of building the kingdom, after he'd gone into heaven. Imagine how they felt.

They probably asked questions such as: 'Can we build it?'

'Yes you can!' God would say, 'Because I'm still with you, and working through you.'

(*Pull the items out of the bag as you tell this story . . .*)

One day Peter and John went to the church (or temple) at three in the afternoon (*clock*). There at the gate was a man who had been paralysed all his life. He couldn't work, so each day he was carried to the gate to beg (*basket*). He'd beg for money from the people who were going into the temple. When he saw Peter and John going past he begged them to give him something. He probably hoped for something like this (*paper money*). But Peter and John looked straight at him and said: 'Look at us! We don't have lots of money' (*empty wallet*). 'But what we have we give you.'

Peter said to him: 'Jesus Christ will make you well.' And Peter helped him up. At once the man's feet and ankles became strong – he jumped to his feet and started to walk around.

Then he went into the temple with them, and danced (*tambourine*), praising God. The people there saw him walking, and recognised him as the beggar who sat at the gate. And they were all amazed at what had happened to him.

End the story by saying how Jesus' friends must have felt about building God's kingdom. They asked the question: 'Can we build it?' The answer was: 'Yes we can – with God's help.' Emphasise that God wants us to work together to get the job done.

Application   Ask the children to think about this a little more, by explaining that there are bits of a jigsaw puzzle around the room. Ask for volunteers to bring the pieces to the front.

(*Put the pieces together*) Does anyone know what it is? A picture of Jesus!

The children will hopefully notice that the hands are missing.

Explain that Jesus has no hands in this world except our hands. Jesus wants to use our hands to build his kingdom here on earth. He wants us to work together with him to get the job done.

Closing prayer

Christ has no body now on earth but yours,
No hands but yours,
No feet but yours;
Yours are the eyes through which to look at
Christ's compassion to the world;
Yours are the feet with which he is
to go about doing good;
Yours are the hands with which he is
to bless us now.

Amen.

(*St Teresa of Avila*)

The Lord's Prayer

Suggested songs

Bob the Builder theme music (EMI/BBC Worldwide Music)
Dear Lord, my Father who's in heaven (The Lord's Prayer)(*Kidsource*)
For I'm building a people (*Kidsource, Junior Praise*)
Go, tell it on the mountain (*BBC Come and Praise 1, Junior Praise*)
Jesus put this song (*Kidsource*)
Make me a channel (*Kidsource, Junior Praise, BBC Come and Praise 2*)
Spirit of God (*BBC Come and Praise 1*)
The building song (*BBC Come and Praise 1*)
The Lord's Prayer (*Junior Praise, BBC Come and Praise 1*) Also to various settings, e.g. Loaves and fishes

Your will be done

Preparation If available, bring in a robot or radio controlled vehicle. Alternatively, bring in something that can be programmed, such as a digital alarm clock or watch.

Bible story As a way in, talk about the programmable object you have brought in and how it responds to your will. If you have an alarm clock, you might like to set it to ring during your talk, saying that it does so because you wanted it to.

Explain that you are going to look at the line of the Lord's Prayer that says:

> Your will be done, on earth as it is in heaven.

Ask the children what they think it means.
Say that in the prayer we are asking for God's will to be done. We're praying: 'God, let your will be done. Not what *I* want, but what *you* want. Lord God, have your way. Let what you want to be done be done through me.'

Encourage the children to think about this further by telling the following traditional story.

A long time ago there were three trees growing together on a hillside. One was an elm, another a beech and the third was an oak. The trees had a good view over the lake below, and as they grew taller people would gather in their shade for rest or for picnics.

Over the years each tree dreamt of what the future might hold. The beech tree loved to look down and watch the people eating their picnics. He loved to watch them open their little picnic boxes revealing food inside. 'I'd like to be a box,' he thought, 'but not just an ordinary box. I'd like to hold something really important. I'd like to hold something so wonderful that people come for miles to see.'

The elm tree also wanted an important job. He liked the fact that people would use the three of them as a meeting place. And if ever people got lost or were separated, they would use the three trees as a way of

Themes
God's will
Prayer
God's instruments

Bible references
Matthew 6:10
Luke 22:39-46
The suggested story about the trees is a traditional one based on old folklore.

finding their way again. 'I'd always like to do that,' the elm tree thought. 'I'd like to be a good signpost, helping people on their journey.'

The oak tree, on the other hand, loved to watch the boats on the lake below. 'Wouldn't it be wonderful,' he thought, 'to be a beautiful yacht and carry important people to all sorts of faraway places.'

Years passed. Then, one day, when the trees were fully grown, men came with axes to cut them down. The tree trunks were sawn into planks of wood and left in a timberyard.

As the months passed, the planks wondered what lay in store for them. Then a man came into the timberyard. He bought the beech-wood in order to build a feeding trough for his animals. 'A feeding trough!' grumbled the beech, 'what sort of a job is that? I want to be a box that holds something important . . . something precious.'

A few years later, a young woman called Mary gave birth to her son, Jesus. She wrapped him in cloths, and carefully laid him in that feeding trough. No box has ever held something so wonderful and precious.

As time went on, two fishermen visited the timberyard. They bought the planks of oak to build their new fishing boat. 'A fishing boat?' thought the oak tree. 'But I don't want to be a smelly fishing boat. What sort of a job is that for me? I want to be a yacht!'

But the oak's wishes did come true. For that fishing boat carried Jesus across the lake a number of times. No yacht has ever had such a privilege.

Still later, a number of Roman soldiers marched into the timberyard. 'We need some planks of elm to make a cross,' they said. 'Do you have any for sale?'

The elm sobbed. All these years he'd dreamt of being a signpost. Now he was going to be made into a cross on which prisoners are put to death. The elm felt terrible. His dream, so he thought, was shattered. The planks of elm were fastened together in the shape of a cross, and on that cross Jesus was crucified.

Although the elm didn't realise it at the time, his wish also came true. For the cross on which Jesus died became a signpost, directing men and women throughout history, the way to God.

Application   Remind the children of the programmable object, saying that it followed your will. Now involve them in the game *Simon says*. The purpose of the game is to show that the children are eager to follow what 'Simon' says, so you need not take the game to its conclusion. As you finish the game, end by saying how eager they were to do what Simon said.

Challenge the children by asking them a question. How eager are we to do what *God* says or wills? If we pray: 'Your will be done' and mean it – it will have an effect on how we live. For there are things that God wants us to do. There are things that God wants us to be. Of course God listens to our prayers and knows what we want. But God loves us very much, and therefore wants what is best for us.

If trees could pray, we know what each tree would pray for.

Closing prayer Christ has no body now on earth but yours,
No hands but yours,
No feet but yours;
Yours are the eyes through which to look at
Christ's compassion to the world;
Yours are the feet with which he is
to go about doing good;
Yours are the hands with which he is
to bless us now.

Amen.

(*St Teresa of Avila*)

The Lord's Prayer

Suggested songs Abba Father (*Kidsource, Junior Praise*)
Dear Lord, my Father who's in heaven (The Lord's Prayer) (*Kidsource*)
Father, I place into your hands (*Junior Praise*)
From heaven you came (*Kidsource*)
I can be what God wants me to be (*Kidsource*)
I want to walk with Jesus Christ (*Junior Praise*)
In days of old (*Kidsource*)
Spirit of God (*BBC Come and Praise 1*)
The Lord's Prayer (*Junior Praise, BBC Come and Praise 1*. Also to various settings, e.g. Loaves and fishes)
We are climbing (*BBC Come and Praise 1*)
We are kingdom kids (*Kidsource*)
You've got to move (*BBC Come and Praise 2*)

Give us this day our daily bread

Preparation

Prepare a large menu with a choice of two or three meals. These could be quite varied and include some pictures. One meal should be very basic (e.g. a bowl of rice, some vegetables, a piece of fruit, and a glass of water). The other meal(s) can be quite fancy, but you might like to include the sorts of food that children like (e.g. chicken nuggets, chips and beans, chocolate fudge cake with ice cream and a glass of cola).

As an aid to telling the story, you might like to place some props in a large bag e.g. a wilting flower, a bird mask or picture, a signpost, a small bag of flour and a thermo-meter. Bring these items out of the bag as you get to the point in the story where they're mentioned.

For the application section you will need five spoons attached to dowel rods or garden canes, and some sweets.

Themes
Elijah and the widow
God provides
Sharing
God's instruments

Bible references
1 Kings 17:8-16 (see also Luke 9:10-17; John 2:1-11)
(Note: The point of this assembly is to show God's understanding of our needs and difficulties, and his delight in working in partnership with us in the provision.)

Bible story

Tell the children that we need quite a lot of food and drink to stay alive. You could use the following statistics. In the UK, by the time the average person reaches 70 years old, they will have eaten 1190 portions of fish and chips; four miles of sausages; 3500 loaves of bread; 2240 bags of crisps; and drunk the equivalent of 60 baths full of milk, and 93,000 cups of tea.

Now show the children the menu, and ask them to choose a meal by a show of hands. Few will choose the basic meal. Explain that the basic meal provides all that we need, whereas the other meal has what we might want. Emphasise the difference, and say how lucky we are in this country in having so much choice.

Tell the children that they are going to hear a story today about a man in the Bible called Elijah. They'll hear that God provided for Elijah's *needs* during a very difficult time. In some places of the world today people have great needs that don't seem to be provided for. That is very sad, because in other parts of the world people have everything they could possibly want and more. If we learnt to share, there'd be enough for everyone.

Ask for five volunteers to stand at the front. (*Pull out the wilting flower from the bag and ask the first volunteer to hold it*) Explain that where Elijah lived there had been no rain for some time. All the plants wilted and it was very difficult to grow food. The rivers began to dry up and soon there would be nothing to drink. How would Elijah find water? How would Elijah eat?

Well, God told Elijah to walk east, and there he found a stream. There was still some water to drink. But what would he eat?

Pull out the *bird mask*, and ask the second volunteer to wear it. Say that God promised to feed Elijah. God told the ravens to bring bits of bread and meat for Elijah to eat every morning and every evening. So God looked after Elijah and kept him safe.

But still the sun shone . . . and Elijah's stream dried up, because there was no rain. Where would Elijah go now?

(*Pull out the signpost*)

'I'll tell you where to go,' God said. So Elijah set off.

He was almost there when he met a poor woman, gathering sticks for her fire.

'I'm very thirsty,' Elijah said – and she went to fetch him some water.

'I'm very hungry too,' he said, calling after her.

(*Pull out the small bag of flour*)

The woman shook her head sadly. 'We have nothing left but a little flour and a drop of oil. My little boy is so hungry. It will be our last meal,' she said. 'And then I don't know what we shall do.'

'Don't worry,' said Elijah. 'Bake me a small loaf first. Then use what is left to bake bread for yourself and for your son. You won't go hungry,' Elijah reassured her. 'God has promised that your flour and oil will not run out until the rain comes. God himself says so.'

The poor woman trusted Elijah. She went away and made some bread for Elijah, for herself and her son. To her amazement she found that there was still some flour and oil left to make bread for the next day.

In fact, there was bread to eat every day. Bread for Elijah, for the woman and for her son, because God was looking after them.

(Pull out the thermometer)

However, some time later, the woman's son became ill. He got worse and worse until he died. The poor woman was very upset and angry that her only son had died. Elijah said: 'Give the boy to me.' He carried the boy upstairs and prayed that God would heal the woman's son. Then the boy started to breathe again. God had answered Elijah's prayer.

Elijah carried the boy downstairs to his mother, and she was so happy. And she said to Elijah 'Now I know that God speaks through you.'

Application End the story by saying that God really is interested in what we need, such as having enough food. That is why, in the Lord's Prayer, Jesus taught us to pray:

Give us today our daily bread.

God is interested in what we need. Refer back to the menu at this point, saying that God provided Elijah with what he needed, not necessarily with what he wanted. God gave Elijah food by sending ravens to feed him. But God also likes to work with people in providing for someone's needs. That's just what the poor woman did. She was very brave, and decided to share all the food that she had with a stranger.

Encourage the children to think about that a little more. Take the props from the children, and give them a long spoon to hold. Tell them that they are to hold the spoons by the end of the long handle and to hold their arms out straight. Place a sweet in each spoon, and tell the children they can eat the sweets, but they're not allowed to bend their arms. See how quickly the children realise that the only way to eat the sweets is for each of them to share with the others.

End by saying that God does provide for us. But he likes us to work with him, and to share what we've been given. If we do that no one need go hungry.

Closing prayer Use the following response in the prayer, with the children saying the words in bold:

Our Lord lives: **God provides everything we need.**

Thank you for food and healthy bodies. **God provides everything we need.**

Thank you for clothes to wear. **God provides everything we need**.

Thank you for friends and family. **God provides everything we need**.

Lord God, you have given us so many wonderful things. Help us to think of ways in which we can share with those who have so little.

Amen.

The Lord's Prayer

Suggested songs

5000+ hungry folk (*Kidsource*)
Dear Lord, my Father who's in heaven (The Lord's Prayer)(*Kidsource*)
Lord of the harvest (*BBC Come and Praise 2*)
Make me a channel (*Kidsource, Junior Praise, BBC Come and Praise 2*)
Mother Teresa's Prayer (*BBC Come and Praise 2*)
My God shall supply all my needs (*Kidsource*)
The Lord's Prayer (*Junior Praise, BBC Come and Praise 1*. Also to various settings, e.g. Loaves and fishes)
Thank you Lord for this fine day (perhaps add some verses e.g. Thank you Lord for giving us food . . . fruit and veg., etc.) (*Junior Praise*)
The sharing bread (*BBC Come and Praise 2*)
When I needed a neighbour (*Junior Praise, BBC Come and Praise 1*)

Forgive us for the bad things we do

Preparation

At the front you will need a tray, a small glass, an empty bottle, red food colouring, clear malt vinegar and some bicarbonate of soda. Put some bicarbonate of soda in the bottle; and mix a teaspoon of red food colouring with the clear vinegar in the glass. You will add the vinegar mixture to the bicarbonate of soda as you talk.

If you have time, you may wish to create a simple volcano . . .

For the application section you will need some clear vinegar in a bowl, two teaspoons of salt, some dirty copper coins and paper towel (lemon juice and even some acidic fizzy drinks could also be used as a substitute for vinegar).

Themes

Forgiveness

A fresh start

Change

Bible references

Matthew 6:14-15; 18:21-35

Luke 6:37-38

Bible story

Ask the children if they have ever seen a volcano erupting on television, or perhaps heard about volcanoes in a lesson. Go on to say that they are actually going to see a volcano in action.

Before a volcano erupts, there is a lot going on under the ground that we can't see. The pressure builds before, all of a sudden, there is a terrific explosion. The pressure forces molten rock and lava out of the volcano, and with it huge amounts of ash and dust.

Explain that at times we can be a bit like a volcano. How? Illustrate with a personal story. Include in the story an element of anger or frustration, and the concept of forgiveness. Alternatively, you might like to tell the story of the unforgiving servant in Matthew 18:21-35.

As you reach a climax in the story, add the vinegar (with red colouring), to the bicarbonate of soda. The resulting mixture will react, producing lots of foam. Explain how we can react quickly out of anger or frustration. We can do things that we shouldn't, and hurt those around us. We can spoil our relationships with family and friends.

Application Ask the children how they might feel if they have fallen out with their friends after an argument. Draw out ideas such as feeling unhappy and feeling dirty on the inside. The good news is that God understands us. He does want us to be like Jesus, to be loving and kind, and to show his love to others. But he knows that sometimes we do things wrong. He knows about our failures, our weakness, the things we do that we shouldn't. God will forgive us if we ask him. Not only will he forgive us, he will also make us feel clean and brand new.

Show the children two copper coins – one shiny, the other dull. It may help to hold the coins near a bright light to emphasise the difference. The coin that looks dull is tarnished. It doesn't feel as nice as a new penny. It doesn't shine anymore. That's what we look like when we've done some things that we shouldn't.

Now place the dull coin into the bowl with the clear vinegar and salt. Say that God wants to forgive us and clean us up. He wants us to feel good and to give us a new start.

The coin will soon look shiny again. Remove it with a spoon, and wipe with paper towel. Hold it up for the children to see. The coin looks like a new one again. For God wants to make us shiny again – to feel new on the inside and the outside.

Hold the cleaned coin in the light. Ask the children if they can see a difference. It's all shiny again. Because when God puts things right, we don't just feel better. We can also shine like a light in the world, reflecting God's goodness. If God forgives us and makes us clean, shouldn't we also forgive those who have hurt us? In that way, we can share God's love with those around us.

That's the end of my story . . .

Closing prayer *Dear God,*

Please help us to be honest with ourselves, with others and with you, by admitting the mistakes we make. Help us to say sorry when we need to.

If there is anything you feel sorry for at the moment, tell God about it quietly now. Ask God to make you clean again.

(Leave space for people to say sorry to God)

Father God, help us to realise that if we are truly sorry for what we have done, the mistakes we make can be forgiven and we can have a fresh, clean start.

Amen.

The Lord's Prayer

Suggested songs
Dear Lord, my Father who's in heaven (The Lord's Prayer) (*Kidsource*)
Give us hope, Lord (*BBC Come and Praise 2*)
God forgave my sin (*Junior Praise*)
Make me a channel (*Kidsource, Junior Praise, BBC Come and Praise 2*)
O Lord, all the world belongs to you (*BBC Come and Praise 1*)
Oh, once there was a father (*Kidsource*)
Peace I give to you (*Junior Praise*)
Some things make you angry (*Kidsource*)
Spirit of God (*BBC Come and Praise 1*)
The Lord's Prayer (*Junior Praise, BBC Come and Praise 1*. Also to various settings, e.g. Loaves and fishes)
The pollen of peace (*BBC Come and Praise 2*)

Keep us from being tempted

Preparation

This outline involves making your own bubble solutions in the assembly. You will require a wire loop (of 2-3cm diameter) with a small handle. These can be made from a pipe cleaner or a large metal paper-clip (alternatively, use the loop from a bought bottle of bubble mixture).

Ingredients and method for first bubble solution

Add ten tablespoons of warm water, followed by one tablespoon of washing-up liquid (one of the top brands works best) to a cup or mug and stir thoroughly. For ease, you may like to have some warm water ready in a thermos.

Ingredients and method for second (improved) bubble solution

Add two heaped tablespoons of white sugar, eight tablespoons of warm water, and one tablespoon of washing-up liquid to a mug and stir thoroughly. The sugar should turn the bubble solution into a syrupy liquid and will add strength to the bubbles.

For the introduction you might also like to have some Harry Potter merchandise on display.

> **Themes**
> Temptation
> Jesus in the wilderness
> Strength from God
>
> **Bible reference**
> Matthew 4:1-11

Bible story

Begin by talking to the children about temptation. You could make a link with Harry Potter. At the start of *Harry Potter and the Chamber of Secrets* (J. K. Rowling: 1998 Bloomsbury Publishing), for example, we are told about Harry's life at Privet Drive. Harry struggles to live with Uncle Vernon and the Dursleys; he feels he doesn't belong. He describes how horribly he's been treated and we learn that the Dursleys even forget Harry's 12th birthday. Yet he constantly strives to do what is right by them. Even when locked in his room with the window barred, Harry tries to do the right thing. Although we can imagine the temptation, Harry does not use his magic to turn the tables on them.

Explain that all of us, whoever we are, will often face temptation. Even Jesus was tempted to do the wrong thing at times. Now tell the children the story of Jesus' temptations in the wilderness. These are Jesus' own special temptations. The Bible tells us, however, that Jesus didn't give in. He managed to resist the temptation and do the right thing.

Now make up the first bubble solution and blow some bubbles. The bubbles will be weak, and you may even have difficulty in creating whole bubbles.

Go on to say that just as Jesus had his own special temptations, so will we. Each of us is weak or vulnerable in some particular way. There are particular things that we would like to do, even though we know they are wrong.

Encourage the children to list (either verbally or on a board at the front) some of the ways in which we can be tempted (e.g. by eating too much; by telling lies; stealing; being selfish).

Blow some more bubbles and emphasise how easily they burst because they are 'weak'.

Go on to say that Jesus was strong and resisted temptation. He can also help us to do the same.

At this point, make up a second solution of bubble mixture. Tell the children that this one will be slightly different. It will contain something extra – something special to make the bubbles strong (make sure that sugar is included as one of your ingredients). Allow the children to see you add the sugar. Stir carefully but thoroughly, so that all the sugar dissolves.

Sugar is like that little extra something that Jesus gives to us when we ask him for help. Try blowing bubbles using the wire loop and notice the difference sugar makes to the strength of the bubbles. You may even like to try a bigger wire loop, and have a couple of volunteers to try and burst them!

Whenever we are tempted, we can put ourselves in God's hands and ask him for help. We can pray: 'Lead us not into temptation', and God will strengthen us and help us to resist.

Closing prayer Go on thinking about that during the day. Next time you are tempted, pray for strength to resist:

Leader: Lord Jesus at times we are all tempted to do the wrong thing. When we are tempted to . . . (*use an example here from the list made by the children*).

All: **Help us to be strong.**

Leader: Lord Jesus, when we are tempted to (*use more examples from your list . . .*)

All: **Help us to be strong.**

Close with the Lord's Prayer.

The Lord's Prayer

Suggested songs   At the name of Jesus (*Junior Praise, BBC Come and Praise 1*)
Dear Lord, my Father who's in heaven (The Lord's Prayer) (*Kidsource*)
In our work and in our play (*Junior Praise*)
Keep me close to you (*Kidsource*)
Let us sing and praise God (*Kidsource*)
One more step (*Junior Praise, BBC Come and Praise 1*)
So if you think you're standing firm be careful (*Kidsource*)
Spirit of God (*BBC Come and Praise 1*)
The Lord's Prayer (*Junior Praise, BBC Come and Praise 1*. Also to various settings, e.g. Loaves and fishes)

Deliver us from evil

Preparation Make five copies or enlargements of the sheep's head (as in diagram). On the back of four, draw the letters **L, O, S** and **T** so that the word *lost* is spelt when they are all held together. On the fifth, write the name Blodders. Before the assembly, stick the five heads randomly around the room. Make sure that the one with Blodders is well hidden (such as behind a door, piano or curtain). You might also like to place some 'sheep merchandise' on a table at the front (e.g. such as Shaun, from *A Close Shave* © Aardman/Wallace & Gromit Ltd.). Party Poppers and confetti will also help your assembly to end with a bang!

Themes
Jesus the good shepherd
God cares for us
Protection from harm

Bible references
Matthew 18:12-14
Luke 15:1-7
Psalm 23
John 10:11-15

Bible story Tell the children that you are looking at the line in the Lord's Prayer which says: 'Deliver us from evil.' It may help to put the words in simpler language, e.g. 'Keep us from all harm.'

Tell the children that you have brought some sheep into school to help with the story, but some have wandered off. Choose volunteers to find four sheep and say that when they've found them they should bring them to the front. Show the children the letters on the back of the sheep and see if they can arrange them to make the word *lost*.

As you begin the story of the good shepherd, you might like to encourage the children to act it out as appropriate (five or six children could link arms to form a sheepfold, for example. With a little adaptation, the sheep heads could also make simple masks. You might even wish to have one or two children acting as wild animals, prowling round the hall).

Story

There was a shepherd with 100 sheep. The shepherd always took great care of his sheep. He always made sure that they had enough grass to eat and water to drink. At night he would lead them home safely to their sheepfold.

Because he was a good shepherd, he would count them in as they went through the gate: 1, 2, 3, 4, 5 . . . and so on, until he reached 96, 97, 98, 99 . . . 100! As a good shepherd he never grew tired of counting his sheep. One night, however, he found that there were only 99. One was lost. Looking around, he soon knew which one was missing . . . it was Blodders.

What did the shepherd do? Did he say to himself: 'I've still got 99 sheep. I'm not going to worry about the one who is lost'? No. Because he was a good shepherd, he was *very* worried. He made sure the rest of the sheep were safe in the fold, and then he set off with his shepherd's stick and club. As he walked he called out 'Blodders', hoping to hear a reply.

Soon it was dark, and the night was full of strange sounds. But the good shepherd still carried on his search, looking in the valleys, among the rocks and bushes (*at this point, begin to walk to where your Blodders is hidden*).

Suddenly the shepherd heard a noise. He gripped the club tightly in his hand, ready to keep any wolves or wild animals away. Something was moving close by. And then . . . (*build up the tension, then reveal your Blodders*) he found Blodders! She was caught in a prickly bush. The shepherd used his stick to get her out. Then he picked her up in his arms, and carried her home on his shoulders.

When Blodders was safely back home, the good shepherd called his friends and said: 'I'm so happy I've rescued my sheep. She is now safe. Let's have a party!' (*Let off the party poppers*)

Application

Tell the children that Jesus told this story in order to show people how much God cares for us. For God is like a good shepherd. He knows us all by name. He knows whether you are called Andrew, Tom, Sarah or Harpreet . . . (*use some children's names relevant to your school here*).

Repeat the line in the Lord's Prayer: 'Deliver us from evil.' Like Blodders, we can sometimes feel weak and helpless. But God knows us and loves us. In the prayer we are asking that God will come and rescue us, just like the good shepherd – that he will keep us from all harm.

Closing prayer   Based on Psalm 23.

The Lord is my shepherd; I have everything I need. He gives me strength. He guides me in the right paths. Even in the deepest darkness I will not be afraid. For God is with me. His shepherd's club and stick keep me safe.

Amen.

Suggested songs   Dear Lord, my Father who's in heaven (The Lord's Prayer) (*Kidsource*)
Father, I place into your hands (*Junior Praise*)
Have you seen the pussycat? (*Junior Praise, Kidsource*)
He's got the whole wide world (*Junior Praise, BBC Come and Praise 1*)
I won't wander off (*Kidsource*)
Jesus is our shepherd (*Kidsource*)
Kum ba yah (*Junior Praise, BBC Come and Praise 1*)
One more step (*Junior Praise, Kidsource, BBC Come and Praise 1*)
The Lord's Prayer (*Junior Praise, BBC Come and Praise 1*. Also to various settings, e.g. Loaves and fishes)
There were ninety-nine sheep (*Kidsource*)
Whenever I'm afraid (*Kidsource*)

For yours is the glory

Preparation   You will need a candle with holder, matches and a small hand mirror. For the introduction you will need three pieces of A3 paper, three felt tips and three blindfolds. For the application section, cut out two people – one from foil the other from card (*if necessary, glue the foil onto card first so that it holds its shape*).

Themes
God's glory
Reflection
Shine as a light in the world

Bible references
Matthew 5:14-16
John 1:4-9; 8:12

Bible story   If possible, begin the assembly in a darkened room. Explain to the children that you are going to look at the line 'For yours is the glory' in the Lord's Prayer.

Ask for three volunteers. Give them a felt tip each and explain that you'd like them to draw a picture in the dark. To make it really dark, blindfold them. Now give them one minute to draw a picture on the paper – perhaps the school, their house or brother or sister. After one minute tell them to stop and take off the blindfolds.

Ask the children what it was like drawing in the dark. Tell the children how important light is. Light helps us to see when we are drawing – it helps us to see what we are doing. It helps us to see where to go, or if we are going wrong. The lights on a car, for example, help the driver to see where they are going at night. The lights help to keep them safe on the road and out of danger.

You could draw further analogies with light. For example, many children like to sleep with a light on at night. The light is reassuring – it helps them to feel safe in the dark.

Light the candle at the front. Allow the children to observe the light for a moment, then read John 8:12, where it says: 'Jesus said: "I am the light of the world".'

What did Jesus mean? Explain that light is often used as a symbol of love, peace and goodness. Jesus was saying that he was just like light. Like light, Jesus helps us to see what we are doing. He helps us to see whether what we are doing is right or wrong. He helps us to see how we are treating others – whether we are being loving or hurtful, kind or selfish. 'Jesus said: "I am the light of the world".'

Now remind the children of the line of the prayer. Glory is a strange word – what does it mean? To help the children discover what it means, hold your mirror behind the candle and let it reflect the light across the room.

Explain that the word glory means reflection. To give glory means to act like a mirror. We give glory to God when we act like a mirror reflecting his goodness and love into the dark corners of the world. We give glory to God when we are kind, loving and thoughtful, like he is. (You may wish to refer to Matthew 5:16 here.)

Application Your figures (made of card and foil) should be a reminder that we are to reflect God in the world, by how we live and by what we say.

Carefully place the cut-out figures behind the candle in turn, and tell the children that the choice is ours (we can be like the foil or the card – shiny, like a mirror, or dull). God wants us to reflect his love in the world. You might like to explain this further by recapping on previous assemblies on the Lord's Prayer. For example, we can reflect God's love by forgiving as we have been forgiven. We can reflect God's love by bringing hope where there is despair. Where there is worry, we can reflect God's goodness in providing for our needs etc.

Closing prayer Use the following response in the prayer:

Lord God, **Glorify your name**.
Lord Jesus, help us to glorify you in our lives. **Glorify your name**.
Where there is doubt let us reflect trust in your promises. **Glorify your name**.
Where there is worry, let us reflect your goodness in providing what we need. **Glorify your name**.
Where there is blame let us reflect your forgiveness. **Glorify your name**.
Where there is despair, let us reflect your goodness. **Glorify your name**.
Lord Jesus, glorify your name in us.

Amen.

Suggested songs Dear Lord, my Father who's in heaven (The Lord's Prayer) (*Kidsource*)
Father, we love you (*Junior Praise*)
Give me oil in my lamp (*Junior Praise, BBC Come and Praise 1*)
Glory (*Kidsource*)
I am a lighthouse (*Junior Praise, Kidsource*)
I'm gonna shine (*Kidsource*)

Jesus is the lighthouse (*Kidsource*)
Light up the fire (*Junior Praise, BBC Come and Praise 1*)
Lord the light of your love (*Kidsource*)
Make me a channel (*Junior Praise*)
The Lord's Prayer (*Junior Praise, BBC Come and Praise 1*. Also to various settings, e.g. Loaves and fishes)
This little light of mine (*Junior Praise, Kidsource*)

How does your garden grow?

Preparation   You will need a simple scene at the front, possibly on a large board (e.g. 1.2 metre by 1.5 metre), showing land, sky and the sun. During the following narrative a picture develops. The added items may be made from coloured paper, or cut from magazines.

Themes
Environment
Caring for God's creation
Working together

Bible reference
Genesis 2:4-15

Bible story   Say that in the beginning God made the world and everything in it. He made the sun and the sky. He made the land and all of the plants and animals. He also made people. And God said to the people: 'I want you to look after all of this. I want you to take good care of it; to protect it and to help it to grow.'

God wants us to work with him to make this world a beautiful place. There are many things we can do to make the world a lovely place to live. Today, let's think of a large garden or park.

First of all, let's plant some trees (*add trees made from newspaper – these can extend upwards to show growth*).

So now we have some lovely trees, hopefully we'll see some birds in our park too (*add bird to tree*), and some animals (*add picture of an animal, depending on what is available e.g. badger, fox, rabbit*).

Let's plant some flowers to make our park more colourful (*add paper flowers to scene*).

But if we want people to enjoy the park, we'd better have some paths for them to walk along (*add a footpath*). Ask for two volunteers – a boy and a girl – to stand by the picture, to represent people in the park.

Now, what will happen to our park if we just leave it? The grass will start to get longer (*add tufts of grass*). Weeds will start to grow (*add some weeds – dandelions etc*). The path will start to wear out (*add some black circles to the path to represent holes*). Some trees may get damaged in strong winds, or become diseased (*bend one of your paper trees across the path*). We may have lots of litter (*add litter to the picture*). It's no longer a nice place to be. It might even be a dangerous place to be. What might happen to the animals with all of this litter on the ground? What might happen if there are holes in the path?

So, once we have made our park, we have to look after it . . . we can't just leave it. Ask the boy and the girl to pick up the litter, and remove the weeds and the tree that has blown down. Ask them to cut the grass (*remove tufts of grass*), and to repair the path (*remove holes on the path*).

Application Emphasise that once we have made our park we have to look after it. The park cannot simply be left. Neither can we leave the task of caring to just one or two. God asks all of us to care for our world. This is what God means when he says: 'I want you to look after all of this. I want you to take good care of the world, to protect it and to help it to grow.'

It is up to us all to care, and to make this a nice world for all to live in. Go on thinking about that during the day.

Closing prayer *Dear God,*

Thank you for the beauty of the world that you have made – for sun and sky, for clouds and trees, for foxes and badgers, cats and dogs. Help us to take good care of all that you have made. Help us to keep this world a beautiful place to live.

Amen.

Suggested songs All things bright and beautiful
Don't know much about the ozone layer (*Kidsource*)
Down in the jungle (*Kidsource*)
I'm going to paint (*BBC Come and Praise 2*)
Think of a world (*BBC Come and Praise 1, Junior Praise*)
What about being old Moses? (*BBC Come and Praise 2*)
When God made the garden of creation (*BBC Come and Praise 1*)
When your Father made the world (*BBC Come and Praise 2*)

Paper Tree

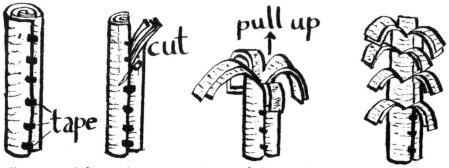

Roll up several sheets of newspaper. Tape as shown. Make cuts in one end. Gently pull insides up and out.

Use it wisely

Preparation This assembly is based on the game *Jenga* or *Jericho* (House of Marbles). In these games players build a tower out of wooden blocks. Once all the available blocks are used, players then take it in turns to remove blocks from anywhere in the tower, and place them on the top. The player who makes the tower collapse is out of the game. Use the same principle to show how fragile the earth is. Say that if we continue to remove vital resources (like the blocks in our game) from the earth, eventually our own way of life will be upset.

> **Themes**
> Environment
> Using the earth's resources wisely
> Sustainable living
>
> **Bible reference**
> Luke 15:11-27

Before the assembly, build a tower. You could use cardboard boxes or kitchen roll tubes. If possible, label the boxes or tubes so that they represent some of nature's resources (e.g. coal, oil, gas and water). Ask children to act out the story.

Bible story There was once a rich man who had two sons. The younger one said: 'Give me my share of your property – now. I want to have some fun.'

That made his father very sad, but he did as the boy asked. A few days later the boy took what his father gave him and got to work.

He dug for coal (*remove the coal block from the tower*). He drilled for gas and oil (*remove the gas and oil blocks*). The boy then used the coal, gas and oil to become very rich (*you could possibly mime selling these to other characters*). The boy was very pleased with himself. He bought himself a fast car. He had many holidays across the world. He had a big house, with an enormous outdoor swimming pool (*remove the water block*). He bought lots of things for his house . . . a television for every room, a video, a DVD player, a CD player, a washing machine . . . (*you may wish to add to the list*). The trouble was, the more he had, the more he wanted. He owned more and more.

At this point in the assembly, allow the tower to collapse. Remove blocks until it does, talking about the boy's extravagance. For example, add that when he no longer liked the colour of his car, he simply bought a new one (*remove an unlabelled block*). When he was tired of his sofa, he bought a new one (*remove another block*). When he wanted a more up-to-date mobile phone, he bought a new one, etc.

After the collapse of the tower, explain that one day his oil well ran dry, his coal was exhausted and he realised how the world had changed from a fruitful world to one laid to waste. He sat amidst the waste, thinking of how things had been at his father's house, and he wondered if it was too late to say sorry.

Application You make like to challenge the children by sharing with them some actual facts about levels of consumption in the UK. For example, in July 2002, a study of the city of York revealed some interesting environmental facts. It showed that 20 per cent of all food bought in the city is thrown away. Thirteen tonnes of CO_2 are produced per person per year in the city, and 100,000 electrical items are bought every year. You could obtain additional facts from the addresses at the back of this book.

Closing prayer For the prayer you might like to lead the children in a time of confession (for an alternative prayer see the *Help! Help!* assembly).
Use the response: '**Father forgive us**' at the end of each line.

We are sorry for plundering the earth's resources without thinking about tomorrow. **Father forgive us**.
We are sorry for the pollution of land, sea and air. **Father forgive us**.
We are sorry for our lack of concern for the health of your world. **Father forgive us**.
We are sorry for thinking only of ways in which we can profit from your creation. **Father forgive us**.

Lord God, heal our relationship with the earth and help us to take care of your creation, in Jesus' name.

Amen.

Suggested songs Don't know much about the ozone layer (*Kidsource*)
Down in the jungle (*Kidsource*)
God in his love (*BBC Come and Praise 2*)
Think of a world (*BBC Come and Praise 1, Junior Praise*)
When God made the garden of creation (*BBC Come and Praise 1*)
When your Father made the world (*BBC Come and Praise 2*)

This assembly is based on an idea by *Eco-congregation*, used with permission.

Help! Help!

Preparation   This story needs little preparation, although it could be acted out using simple props. One idea is to dress Ms Glo Ball (the planet Earth) in colours to represent the four elements (earth, water, wind and fire). Twigs and a few leaves could also be pinned onto the outfit. The politician and businessman or woman could walk on with a small briefcase, umbrella, sunglasses or hat. Alternatively, tell the story with puppets. These can be made from basic materials (e.g. kitchen roll tubes for the main body, with buttons for eyes etc.). Another idea, possibly as a follow-up to the assembly, would be to litter-pick the area around the school (with adult supervision) and use the items found to make a frieze to illustrate the theme of caring for the environment.

Themes
Conservation
Commitment to care for the planet
Green goals

Bible reference
Luke 10:25-37

Bible story   Our story begins one day when Ms Glo Ball was walking down a lonely road. All of a sudden some big, bad robbers jumped out. 'Help! Help!' cried Ms Glo Ball – but there was no one to hear her cry.

(Characters mime a fight. Hold up a large 'Biff-Pow' sign in front of the characters and shout Stop!)

You get the general idea.

Ms Glo Ball was badly hurt and fell (*gently!*) to the ground. The robbers took what they could and ran away.

'Oh! Oooh!' groaned Ms Glo Ball, lying at the side of the road. She hurt all over. She couldn't get up. She lay there in the burning sun, unable to do anything.

Now it just so happened that Mr Carryon, the politician, was driving past in his flashy car (*child mimes being in a car*). He stopped his car and got out. Ms Glo Ball thought: 'I'm going to be all right. He'll listen and give me some help.'

But Mr Carryon the politician said: 'I didn't stop the car to help you. I stopped to go to the loo.' (*Momentarily turns back on audience, mimics zipping up trousers, then turns to the front again and gets into car).* And off he went on his way.

In the same way, Mr D. Seever, the businessman, came past.

'Ello,' he said. 'What's this then?'

Ms Glo Ball could only groan . . . 'Oooh!'

'Tut tut,' said Mr D. Seever: 'You won't get any sympathy from me. You need to get up and pull yourself together,' and without looking too closely, Mr D. Seever walked on past without stopping to help.

But then some people from *x* school (*use name of school*) happened to be travelling the same way, and they saw Ms Glo Ball lying there in the road, wounded.

(Have the volunteers walk to the Earth. Shout: 'STOP!')

Now involve all the children. Ask them what their response might be to Ms Glo Ball (the Earth). Would they simply ignore the wounded Earth and carry on their journey, like the politician or businessman, or would they stop to help? What could they do to help her get better? In the Bible there's a story of a Good Samaritan traveller who stopped to help, and it cost him personally. Draw a parallel by saying that when we seek to help the Earth it may cost us personally (e.g. we may have to walk to school or take items for recycling rather than just throw them in the bin). Leave the story there and say that the ending depends on us.

Application　Encourage the children to think about each of the characters in the story. Who are we like? Are we like Mr Carryon or Mr D Seever, who do not want to be concerned with the cost of caring for the world? Or will we be the one to stop and help? We should not ignore our hurting world. God asks all of us to care, and to make this a nice world for all to live in.

Closing prayer　*Dear God,*

We thank you for the beauty of the earth. Thank you for the majestic mountains, lush green vales, mighty oaks and beaming buttercups. We are sorry that we have turned it into mountains of waste, valleys of landfill, depleting resources and forgetting tomorrow. Help us, instead, to bring healing for the earth, so that future generations may enjoy your creation.

Amen.

Suggested songs   Don't know much about the ozone layer (*Kidsource*)
Down in the jungle (*Kidsource*)
From the tiny ant (*BBC Come and Praise 2*)
I was lying in the roadway (*BBC Come and Praise 2*)
Jesus' hands were kind hands (*Kidsource*)
Sun and the moon and the starlit sky (*Kidsource*)
Think of a world (*BBC Come and Praise 1, Junior Praise*)
When your Father made the world (*BBC Come and Praise 2*)

Resources

Decade Ministries	Many resources available (e.g. story bags, printed rolls for teaching the Lord's Prayer/Christmas and Easter stories). Telephone and fax: 01488 71077 E-mail: roy@decadeministries.co.uk
Eco-congregation	The Churches' Environmental Programme c/o The Arthur Rank Centre, National Agricultural Centre, Stoneleigh Park, Warwickshire. CV8 2LZ Telephone: 024 76 858 347 Website: www.ecocongregation.org (free resources available) E-mail: enquiries@encams.org
Furryland Crafts	Animal puppets for assemblies and children's work. 6 Steeplands, Bradley, Huddersfield. HD2 1QQ. Telephone and fax: 01484 532270 Website: www.furryland.co.uk
Jairus' Daughter	A musical by Roger Jones © 1992. Many musicals available (e.g. *David*). Published by Christian Music Ministries, 325 Bromford Road, Hodge Hill, Birmingham. B36 8ET. Telephone: 0121 783 3291 Website: www.cmm.org.uk E-mail: sales@cmm.org.uk
Kidsource	Songs for church and school. Compiled by Capt. Alan Price, CA. Published by Kevin Mayhew Ltd (1999).
Loaves & Fishes	An all-age setting for the Lord's Supper. By Susan Sayers and Colin Mawby © (2002). Published by Kevin Mayhew Ltd.
'Naughty Cecil'	A counting song produced by K Bolam. CD and Cassette released 2001 by Marks & Spencer PLC ©
Praying as Jesus Taught Us	(Sixteen services reflecting the Lord's Prayer) By Susan Sayers © 2002. Published by Kevin Mayhew Ltd.
Puppet Resources	Ian and Elaine Coules, 34 Ashfield, Liverpool. L15 1EZ. Telephone: 0151 733 4647
The Very Hungry Caterpillar	By Eric Carle © 1974. Puffin Books.